D0596765

"Oh, how I wish I'd had this book when I became a single mom fourteen years ago! Sandra Aldrich sees straight into my heart and shares an honest, transparent look into her own life. She tackles the emotional, spiritual, financial, and parental challenges of single motherhood with reality, humor, and grace and provides a perfect blend of practical tips and warm encouragement. Be sure to share these heart hugs with every single mom you know."

Mary Jo Tate, author of *Flourish: Balance for Homeschool Moms*

Heart Hugs

for

Single Moms

52 Devotions *to* Encourage You

Sandra Picklesimer Aldrich

Revell
a division of Baker Publishing Group
Grand Rapids, Michigan

© 2015 by Sandra Picklesimer Aldrich

Published by Revell
a division of Baker Publishing Group
P.O. Box 6287, Grand Rapids, MI 49516-6287
www.revellbooks.com

Excerpts taken from *From One Single Mother to Another*, © 1991 by Regal Books.

Printed in the United States of America

All rights reserved. No part of this publication may be reproduced, stored in a retrieval system, or transmitted in any form or by any means—for example, electronic, photocopy, recording—without the prior written permission of the publisher. The only exception is brief quotations in printed reviews.

Library of Congress Cataloging-in-Publication Data is on file at the Library of Congress, Washington, DC.

ISBN 978-0-8007-2660-7

Unless otherwise indicated, Scripture quotations are from the Holy Bible, New International Version®. NIV®. Copyright © 1973, 1978, 1984, 2011 by Biblica, Inc.™ Used by permission of Zondervan. All rights reserved worldwide. www.zondervan.com

Scripture quotations labeled KJV are from the King James Version of the Bible.

15 16 17 18 19 20 21   7 6 5 4 3 2 1

In keeping with biblical principles of creation stewardship, Baker Publishing Group advocates the responsible use of our natural resources. As a member of the Green Press Initiative, our company uses recycled paper when possible. The text paper of this book is composed in part of post-consumer waste.

To my son and daughter, Jay and Holly.

Thanks, kiddos, for keeping me from running away to Tahiti—or Kentucky—at the beginning of my singlehood and for giving me many reasons to see the joy in each new day.

Your grateful single mother

Contents

Contents

Acknowledgments

During those early years of finding my own footing in the new role as a single mother, I gleaned information from other single mothers as they told me of their challenges and victories. Thus, it is my privilege to include some of their experiences in these pages. And in appreciation of the trust they've shown me, I've changed most of their names to protect their privacy. Special thanks go to my sister Thea Picklesimer for sharing her insights. Her encouraging calls arrive when I need them most.

God's Word continues to encourage me in this journey, so each devotion begins with Scripture that has helped me during tough days. The quotation for Day 1 is from the King James Version, but the remaining verses are from the New International Version. My concern isn't which translation you prefer, but that you will allow our heavenly Father to speak to you and guide you through his Word.

Everyone at Revell, a division of Baker Publishing Group, deserves one of my Kentucky hugs, but several folks went out of their way to encourage this project: Kim Bangs, Senior Acquisitions Editor for Bethany House and Chosen; Mary Wenger, Managing Editor; Twila Bennett, Executive Director of Marketing and Publicity; Cheryl Van Andel, Senior Art Director; Janelle Mahlmann, Assistant Marketing Manager; and Claudia Marsh, Publicist. God bless you all.

A Welcoming Hug

Day 1

Different Tickets, Same Boat!

> Woe is me for my hurt! my wound is grievous; but I said,
> Truly this is a grief, and I must bear it. Jeremiah 10:19 KJV

The book you are holding is written by this single mother to encourage and help you, no matter your status as a single mom.

I was thrust into single parenting when my children, Jay and Holly, were ten and eight. Today, both are college graduates, employed, happily married, and fully responsible adults. And neither sold drugs, stole cars, or turned out to be an ax murderer.

I say that to encourage you, especially if you are new to single parenting. Too often if we listen to the media, we fear for our children's futures. After all, we hear the tragic stories featuring those raised in one of the fourteen million single-parent homes in the United States.

But even though those numbers are high, our children are not statistics. So don't listen to your fears and don't lose hope because of scary media reports. Listen instead to the Lord and draw on your own God-given strength. You *can* walk this path and you *can* arrive at the finish line—not only as a survivor but as a victor.

I confess I never expected to write about single parenting. After all, my plans included taking care of my family, being a good cook, and creating fun holidays while teaching full-time. Parenting children on my own just wasn't part of the deal. Thus, I've learned far more than I ever wanted to know about being a single mother since that December afternoon when brain cancer defeated my husband and spun me into a role I had not wanted and had not planned on. The following devotions, however, feature not my widowhood but the common struggles and victories we share as single mothers—whether widowed or divorced; raising grandchildren or having adopted; married with husbands absent because of military duty, prison, illness, or addiction; or never married but having chosen giving birth and parenting instead of abortion.

You can walk this path and you can arrive at the finish line—not only as a survivor but as a victor.

Yes, each status carries specific challenges, but no matter how we came on board, we all are in the same boat. So let's encourage each other.

When my husband died, everyone hovered around me—for two weeks—whispering, "Oh, you poor dear." But when several of my friends had divorce thrust upon them or had to choose it to protect themselves and their children from terrible abuse, some of them were treated like lepers. Yes, grief from death is a deep cut, but it's a clean cut. The grief that accompanies many other single-parenting situations is deep and jagged.

I also want to encourage those never-married mothers who have bravely rejected the option of abortion. They have determined, with God's help and with that of family and friends, to raise their children themselves. If you are one of those mothers, let me thank you for not aborting your child. God is not finished with any of us yet. And I am convinced he will bring his good out of your wise, and perhaps sacrificial, decision.

And before we go any further, I need to get one of my pet peeves out of the way: people who constantly refer to single-parent families as "broken homes." Many of us feel that through God's help and a great deal of personal effort, our homes are healed, even if that healing didn't come overnight. Know, then, if you're a recent single mom and juggling far too many responsibilities alone, I understand some of what you're dealing with. Much of the spiritual and practical counsel I offer through these pages I've learned the hard way—by living through it. But I won't try to advise you on how to raise perfect youngsters. I never figured out how to do *that* myself. I simply pray you will be encouraged that you and your children *do* have bright tomorrows.

Grief from death is a deep cut, but it's a clean cut. The grief that accompanies many other single-parenting situations is deep and jagged.

Perhaps you muttered, "Yeah, sure," when you read the previous statement. Let me assure you that you *are* stronger than you think. In those first, early days of my own singlehood, I couldn't look ahead to where I am now. But while thinking, and worrying, about my single-parenting role, I looked to the examples of strong women in the Bible and in my own family.

I wanted to be like Anna of Luke 2:36–37, the widow who had served in the temple for most of her adult life. But, unlike Anna, I couldn't withdraw from the world. Economics wouldn't let me, and my children needed me.

I thought too of Molly Pitcher, the woman who carried water to wounded and dying men during the Revolutionary War. Her real name was Mary Ludwig Hays, but as the men used her nickname and called, "Molly! Pitcher!" she gained the name that stuck.

During one particularly fierce battle, she saw her husband fall beside the cannon he was firing. She ran to his side, not to cradle him in her arms, but to take his place and fire the cannon!

I wanted to be that type of woman! But I had learned early that such personal strength alone can't conquer all situations.

My great-grandmother Mintie Farley, whom I remember, often related stories of the craziness surrounding the Civil War—or as it more correctly should be called, "The War Between the States." Anyway, she said all the men in their little Kentucky community had gone to war, leaving their wives and children alone on the hillside farms. Her mother, Minerva, was one of those wives. Both Union and Confederate armies repeatedly crossed Kentucky, so first one army and then another had stolen everything edible. Minerva had begged to keep one milk cow and a couple of chickens for the sake of her children, but soldiers merely laughed. Then one afternoon more men stormed in, demanding the food they were convinced was hidden. Minerva squared her shoulders and said everything was gone. But an officer pointed his pistol at her head and said it would be a shame to kill her in front of the children. Of course, she gave the soldiers the last of the food. How did she and her children survive after that? On boiled weeds and small critters she captured with homemade traps.

> *Molly ran to his side, not to cradle him in her arms, but to take his place and fire the cannon! I wanted to be that type of woman!*

Over the years, the family story was retold so much and became so real to me I could have reported the color of the officer's hair. As I'd express my indignation, my grandmother Mama Farley would say, "Honey, there are some things in life that all you can do with 'em is bear 'em."

Well, I don't want to *bear* situations. I want them fixed. Now. And in my way. So learning to bear singleness with grace didn't come overnight, and, human being that I am, I've made plenty of mistakes along the way. I'm much stronger now, but it has taken prayer and personal pep talks to get to this peaceful point. And I'm convinced you will get here too. How? By hanging on to the Lord and putting one foot in front of the other. So for now, imagine that I'm putting an arm around your weary shoulders as I say, "Honey, you *can* do this."

Prayer: Father God, you know my situation. You know my fears. Help me feel your presence during this awful time. Help me recognize my own God-given strength even as I ask for your moment-by-moment guidance.

Thoughts to Ponder

1. What are your greatest fears?
2. What are your greatest strengths?
3. What examples of strong women—from the Bible, history, or your own family—do you appreciate most?

Personal Ponderings

The Single-Parent Tightrope

Don't Quit Now!

I will say of the LORD, "He is my refuge and my fortress, my God, in whom I trust." Psalm 91:2

Many of us single mothers find ourselves in a life we did not plan, were not prepared for, and did not want. And even if you chose single motherhood through adoption or by rejecting abortion, you still find yourself facing unexpected challenges. Yes, most of us pictured a life far different from the way it has turned out.

Occasionally, a married friend asks me what single parenting is like. I describe a tightrope strung across a deep gorge. A single parent—in this case, a young mother—gingerly walks across the rope, concentrating on the numerous balls she's juggling. Some have labels: "child care" or "work" or "debt" or "health." Perhaps even "rejection" and "custody battles" are included, but always she's worrying about keeping all those balls in the air.

On each side of the gorge run folks clamoring for her attention—children, relatives, bosses, friends. Then one smooth-talking type beckons for her to step off the rope. At places where the rope dips close to the stony path where he stands, it would be easy for her to drop all those balls and join him. But she continues on, looking only at the responsibility coming down toward her hand at the moment, knowing if she looks away, she can lose her balance.

Often as I describe this scene, my married friend will take a deep breath and say, "Oh, I hope I never have to face that. I wouldn't survive."

My response is simple: "I never thought I would either. But we conquer challenges by putting one foot in front of the other while we hang on to the Lord."

We single mothers know about frightening challenges. In fact, just hours into my own single parenting, I clutched my hands together as I confided to my friend Darlene that I was overwhelmed by all the tasks swarming toward me. Darlene put her hand on my arm and said, "Keep the children clean and fed. The rest will fall into place."

"Keep the children clean and fed. The rest will fall into place."

Her gentle, wise directive calmed me and pulled me back from panic's abyss. And gradually, I learned she was right about the other tasks. Surprises were still ahead, though.

My daughter, Holly, was in third grade when she came home one day in tears. The room mother had handed out directions to an event and said, "Take these home to your families."

Then she'd glanced at Holly and said, "Sorry. I mean to your *moms*."

In our Michigan kitchen, my eight-year-old sobbed as she said, "I want to be a family again." I put my arm around her. "Holly, we are still a family," I said. "We're just a family of *three* now."

She leaned against me in relief. That was a turning point for both of us.

That incident, along with others, made me realize that if we were going to survive as a family, we'd have to fight unexpected emotional battles along the way. And the only way my kiddos could develop their own strength was by watching me.

As I share what I learned, please understand I have no perfect solutions—and beware of anyone who says they have all the answers.

But I can tell you what has worked, or didn't work, for me and for the other single mothers who shared their experiences with me. And remember, whatever successes and achievements came our way rarely were the result of any personal innate wisdom. As a rule, they came because of grace on God's part and much trial and error on ours.

This I know for sure, though: All women raising children alone have too much stress, too many responsibilities, and too little time. And none of us has an identical family situation or face the identical concerns of any other single mom. So as you read my smorgasbord of various dos and don'ts, select those ideas and options you feel will benefit you and your family. And then cheerfully ignore the rest.

> *"Holly, we are still a family," I said. "We're just a family of* three *now."*

I realize the world has changed rapidly, often to the point of seeming to spin out of control. But whether single parenting arrived on the mid-1800s Oregon Trail, in the 1920s Kentucky coal camps, or just last week, it is filled with hurdle after hurdle. In my own life, I didn't have a clue how I was going to handle everything single mothers have to do. I had married young and gone from my childhood home to a college apartment complex. And even though I'd taught in a Detroit suburban school and had handled numerous professional duties, I knew nothing about paying bills, budgeting, balancing a checkbook, doing home maintenance, or repairing a car. Those had been among my husband's responsibilities.

So how could I raise two children to be healthy adults without their father? How could I teach my ten-year-old son to be a man? Even an extended family filled with uncles and cousins did not offer a close-at-hand male relative who could provide the father figure Jay would need.

So I worried and prayed a lot in those first years. I kept us all in church and trusted those couple of hours each week would provide both my children with glimpses of what true manhood is like.

Since his dad's death, Jay's grown up with a mother, a sister, and a neutered cat. Yet he has turned into a masculine, responsible young man.

As I've said before, I didn't know the good outcome in those early days. I knew only that I couldn't quit. And whenever weariness or frustration caused me to forget that God brings his good out of whatever we give him, something would happen to encourage me. Sometimes it was a Bible verse seemingly aimed right at me. Other days it was a friend's comment. And sometimes it even was a goofy experience—such as the Saturday when my writing wasn't going well. That day my most persistent thought seemed to be, *Whatever made me think I could write?*

So how could I raise two children to be healthy adults without their father? How could I teach my ten-year-old son to be a man?

Unexpectedly in the middle of that sluggish morning, Holly, by then a student at a nearby college, arrived home and insisted we go horseback riding.

"Might as well," I muttered. "I'm not getting anything else accomplished."

Within the hour, we were at our favorite stable here in the Colorado mountains, but the docile brown horse I usually rode was already on the trail for the entire day. That gentle horse had two speeds—slow and stop—so I was disappointed he wasn't available. There was nothing to do but request the *second* most docile horse. When a large black horse was brought out, we eyed each other for a moment, then I took the reins and led him to the mounting block. There, I placed my left foot in the stirrup and had just started to swing my right leg over the saddle when the horse decided he didn't want me on his back. And he cleverly, and quickly, began to sidestep away from the block. There I was, one foot in the stirrup and the other poised in midair. Even back then I didn't have the agility, nor the dainty figure, to shift my weight quickly and throw myself into the saddle. Instead, I was perched in midair for several moments.

The stable owner danced back and forth below me, arms in the air as though to catch me when I fell. There was only one convenient part of my anatomy to push, but he knew me well enough to know he better not touch that. So with arms waving, he hopped from foot to foot and yelled, "Don't quit *now*, ma'am! Don't quit now!"

Holly was bent forward in her own saddle, howling with laughter at the scene, so of course, I started chuckling and then had an even tougher time hauling myself into position. But finally, with a surge of adrenaline, I shifted my weight and shoved my right foot into the stirrup.

The horse gave a defeated snort as I tugged on the reins and followed a laughing Holly up the trail. That ride, even with its tenuous start, proved to be exactly what I needed to finish the wearisome writing assignment. In addition, it has since provided an extra push when I'm tempted to give up. So please hear me as I shout from this page, "Don't quit now!" I'm convinced good days *are* ahead for you too.

Prayer: *Father God, thank you for walking with me as I juggle my many responsibilities as a single mother. Thank you for reminding me, "Don't quit now!" Thank you for showing me that through you, I have greater strength than I ever imagined.*

Thoughts to Ponder

1. What are your many responsibilities? Which are the most challenging?
2. How do you maintain a sense of family with your children?

3. What helps you put one foot in front of the other when you're tempted to quit?

Personal Ponderings

_____

_____

_____

Day 3 · Roll Away the Stone
Trust the Lord for the Impossible

I can do all this through him who gives me strength. Philippians 4:13

I'm originally from Harlan County, Kentucky, and grateful for my strong Appalachian heritage. But even as I set my jaw and turn toward the next challenge, I occasionally still struggle with feelings of inadequacy. Sometimes I'm even tempted to call myself stupid—especially when I don't get the hang of something as quickly as I had hoped.

In those moments, I replay the mental tapes of every mistake I've ever made. But over the years, I've learned I'm not the only single mother who's ever struggled with self-esteem issues. I've also learned that every time we mentally beat ourselves up, we're helping the Enemy. And he's one turkey I'm not at all interested in helping any more than I already have in life.

The feeling of being inadequate was especially strong early in my singlehood as I considered the "what ifs" and "if onlys." For encouragement I turned to the Bible. Sure enough, I was strengthened as I read about women such as Deborah, Ruth, and Esther, who faced impossible situations but were victorious. Soon I was personalizing everything I read in the Scriptures. One of my favorite accounts is in John 11—the raising of Lazarus from the dead. Early in the story, Mary and Martha of Bethany sent word to Jesus that his dear friend, their brother Lazarus, was very ill.

> *Our Lord will give us the strength to handle our responsibilities as we keep putting one foot in front of the other and don't give up or give in to fear.*

Jesus deliberately stalled, though, until his friend had died. When he finally arrived in Bethany, he went to the grave and told the men nearby to roll away the stone to Lazarus's tomb.

Then he said in a loud voice, "Lazarus, come out!" (John 11:43).

I'm fascinated Jesus had to say, "*Lazarus*, come out!" I'm convinced since he is Life, every grave would have given up its dead if he had shouted a mere, "Come out!"

When Lazarus emerged from the tomb, he still was bound by grave clothes. Then Jesus said to those standing nearby, surely with their mouths hanging open, "Take off the grave clothes and let him go" (v. 44).

How's that again? The One who raised a man from the dead was asking others to roll away stones and untie grave clothes? I'm convinced one reason was to make a visual point: We are to do what we can and trust God for the outcome. Even these years later, I'm relieved at the implication for single mothers: Our Lord will give us the strength to handle our responsibilities as we keep putting one foot in front of the other and don't give up or give in to fear. It's like the old adage says, "Pray as though everything depends on God, and work as though everything depends on you."

I hope you are claiming specific Scripture as your own. But if not, today is a good time to start. Philippians 4:19 is a verse I claimed early as a single mother: "But my God shall supply all your need according to his riches in glory by Christ Jesus" (KJV).

Many times I tested that promise and challenged him with "Even *this* need, God?" Gradually, I learned he hadn't overlooked anything. As I learned to pray about every challenge and every decision, he always answered, though not always as I had hoped. Sometimes he used friends to show me how to change the oil in the car or how to balance the checkbook. Sometimes he encouraged me through a glorious sunset and with the constant thought that he was with us and guiding me through the rough spots of single parenting.

Another encouraging verse I clung to in those early days is Isaiah 54:5—"For your Maker is your husband—the LORD Almighty is his name—the Holy One of Israel is your Redeemer; he is called the God of all the earth."

If you believe that verse too then we share the same husband, you and I, and I'm not jealous! This verse gave me special comfort early on because before single parenting I'd never made a major decision by myself. I was terrified a wrong choice would jeopardize my children's future, so I prayed about everything, asking for clear direction.

Along the way I learned it is okay to argue with the Lord a little. I remember the day I could no longer ignore the burned-out recessed lightbulb in the family room's high ceiling. Sigh. Time to drag out the tall ladder. Perched on one of the narrow steps, I started complaining to God. His shoulders are pretty big, and he knows what we're thinking anyway, so he can handle our honesty. Besides, when Jesus said, "Come unto me," he did *not* add, "Come with a smile on your face." Or even "Come without tears." He just said, "Come."

So I told my Husband, God of the Universe, that *husbands* are supposed to change lightbulbs and I shouldn't have to do this. From there, my complaining quickly progressed to, "I shouldn't have to do this single-parenting thing either."

When I was finished whining, I had the good sense to be quiet and listen. In that moment, it was just as though he said, "Try turning it the other way."

When Jesus said, "Come unto me," he did not add, "Come with a smile on your face." Or even "Come without tears." He just said, "Come."

Try turning it the other way? But I know the lightbulb changing rule. It's righty-tighty, lefty-loosey. But my way wasn't working, so I gave the bulb a half-hearted turn the other way. And it fell right into my hand!

As I examined the bulb, I could see the base had been damaged—perhaps as the previous owner had forced the bulb into place. God knew the threads of the lightbulb were damaged, just as he knows those areas of my life where I am the weakest. As I stared at the old bulb, I determined to trust even greater areas of my life and my family to him.

Prayer: Father God, I know about being inadequate. And at times, I identify more with the dead Lazarus than I do the risen one. But even as I confess that, I know you understand the areas of my life that are damaged, just like Sandra's lightbulb. So help me trust you and feel your presence in new ways.

Thoughts to Ponder

1. Do you ever struggle with low self-esteem? If so, what helps?
2. What is your reaction to Jesus waiting until Lazarus died before he went to Bethany?

3. Do you identify with the scenario about changing the damaged lightbulb? Why or why not?

Personal Ponderings

Day
4

Dinner Guests and Angels

Sharing Special Times

For he will command his angels concerning you to guard you in all your ways; they will lift you up in their hands, so that you will not strike your foot against a stone. Psalm 91:11–12

Personalizing Scripture helped me tackle unfamiliar responsibilities, but I knew from my teaching experiences that my children still needed a routine to govern homework, meals, chores, and bedtimes. Familiar structure would conquer daily chaos and add organization and even peace to our routines. And if single parents need anything, it's peace. One habit that helped add peace to our days was reading short Scripture passages together, even when we had guests.

One evening Holly's friend, Jessica, and Jay's German friend, Till, were with us. After we finished our meat-loaf supper, Jay read a few psalms. I turned to Jessica and Till, explained it was our custom to take turns praying, and said they were welcome to join us.

Till nervously replied, "But I've never prayed in English!"

"Then pray in German," I said. "You're talking to God, not to us. But you don't have to pray aloud if you don't want to. You do whatever makes you feel comfortable."

> *Psalm 91:11 says angels will guard us. But it wasn't until I was on a church tour when we lived in Michigan that I learned firsthand God wasn't kidding.*

So Jay prayed first, followed by Jessica and Holly. I was all set to close the prayers when Till hesitantly began to pray. In his first timid words, I caught the word *Deutsch* and knew he was telling the Lord I'd said he could pray in German.

Gradually, his timidity slipped away, and he began to earnestly talk to God. Even though I couldn't understand the words, I understood the emotion and felt the thankfulness welling up within his prayer.

We would have missed a special blessing that evening if we had discarded our family routine because of fear about what guests might think. And often having Jay's and Holly's friends at our table provided opportunities to discuss all sorts of topics, including one time when I was asked whether I believe angels show up today on earth.

I do believe angels are among us. After all, Psalm 91:11 says angels will guard us. But it wasn't until I was on a church tour when we lived in Michigan that I learned firsthand God wasn't kidding.

On that tour, I'd wandered away from the hotel where the group was resting that afternoon and had walked for perhaps an hour. Then as I sat on a low wall to get my bearings, I discovered I was unwelcome. Someone threw stones at me from behind a nearby fence.

Oh, dear, I thought. I told myself the stones were being thrown by an obnoxious kid who would take pleasure in any fear I displayed. But I also realized I couldn't have come up with anything more thoughtless than walking alone in unfamiliar territory. I took a deep breath.

"Well, Lord, this isn't the brightest thing I've done," I told him. "But I thank you for the promise that angels are watching over me." I took another deep breath and added specifics to my prayer. "Now I'd like one special angel to walk beside me. And since angels can take any form they want, I'd like him to be big and visible to anyone whose heart is evil."

I imagined my personal angel as about six foot eight and 290 pounds, with his longish brown hair held back with a don't-mess-with-me bandana.

I imagined my personal angel as about six foot eight and 290 pounds, with his longish brown hair held back with a don't-mess-with-me bandana. I even nicknamed my angel "Buddy." Then I stood up, ignored the stones falling around me, and walked confidently back to the hotel with my celestial escort beside me.

When I returned home and picked up Jay and Holly from their grandparents' home, I told them about the event, adding the usual admonishment that we aren't to test God by foolishly taking risks. Jay nodded, but ten-year-old Holly quickly took to the idea of angels' care. Thus, when we moved to New York a while later, she asked, "If Buddy's with us in the hotel, who's gonna watch the truck with our furniture?"

So I created Buddy's twin brother, "Buford." I described how he would stand outside the truck, leaning against it and cleaning his fingernails with a pocket knife.

If any kids snooped around the truck, he'd quietly come around the side of the vehicle and say, "I reckon you boys better go someplace else."

Holly smiled and quickly fell asleep. Then in the middle of the night, two drunks were fighting in the hallway outside our room. The noise awakened me, of course, and I quietly prayed as I reached for the phone to alert the front desk. But before I could place the call, I heard two security personnel breaking up the fight and sending the drunks to their separate rooms. The next morning, I casually asked Jay and Holly if they'd heard the fight. Jay, who could sleep through anything back then, shrugged. Holly's answer surprised me, though. She said the commotion had awakened her, but she figured Buddy was the one making all the noise in the hallway as he protected us. And she merely had turned over and gone back to sleep!

Being a Kentuckian, I'm sure *Appalachian* angels watched over us during that move. The theology here may be shaky, but Buddy and Buford helped my frightened young daughter—and her mother—sleep well.

How about you? What do you do when you and your family need extra protection? Buddy and Buford have plenty of celestial cousins, so invite them along.

Prayer: Father God, we do need your peace in our busy days. Help me include prayer in our busy schedule. And help me as I ponder the thought that angels truly are among us. May I be open to yet another of your ways of protecting my family.

Thoughts to Ponder

1. Are you comfortable sharing your family routine and faith with guests? Why or why not?
2. What's your reaction to the account of angels named Buddy and Buford?
3. Have you ever been in a situation where you needed God's protection? If so, what happened?

Personal Ponderings

Unrealistic Expectations

Day 5

Others Can't Be All We Need

But now, Lord, what do I look for? My hope is in you. Psalm 39:7

Most of us learned a long time ago that we can't expect others to be all we need. But we keep hoping, don't we? I remember one young single mother who demanded the men of the church answer her every call for help. If her car tires needed air or if her house windows were dirty, she called on the churchmen to assist her. When they balked—after all, most of them didn't wash windows for their *own* wives!—she complained to the pastor, saying the church was supposed to take care of its widows.

That's true, but only to a point. The instructions in James 1:27 direct the church "to look after orphans and widows in their distress." That includes providing shelter and food, but not taking over work they can—and should—do themselves.

And we can't expect others to take on our hurt. Even though it's been several years since her divorce, Judy still holds a grudge against a woman in her church who didn't respond to the news the way Judy felt she should have.

In great detail, Judy describes the Wednesday night service when her husband handed her the car keys, said, "Who are we trying to kid?" and walked out. In that moment, she knew their struggling marriage was over. Numb, she sat through the rest of the service, wanting to give him enough time to walk the few blocks home, pack his suitcase, and leave.

> *Let's welcome the help when it comes, but let's not demand it.*

After the service, the woman sitting behind her asked if everything was all right. With tears running down her cheeks, Judy blurted out she was facing a divorce.

"Then the woman patted my arm, muttered God would be with me, and went home with *her* husband!" Judy says.

Sure, it would have been wonderful if the woman had wrapped Judy in a hug and said, "Oh, honey!" But she didn't.

If we're going to think, *It's not fair* and be hurt every time someone fails to provide what we think we need, we're going to be hurting a lot. Other people have their own problems, and they can't take on ours any more than we can take on theirs. So let's welcome the help when it comes, but let's not demand it. By looking at our situation realistically, we can get through it with less disappointment—and less bitterness.

Please understand that I'm not trying to pour more discouragement into your life. After all, I've learned from personal experience how difficult being a single mom is. Yes, we'd love to have a pat on the shoulder occasionally, but I've also learned that longing for encouragement and praise takes energy better used in tending to the duties at hand. Remember, the ancient Greeks awarded the prize not to the winner who crossed the finish line first but to the one who finished first *with his torch still burning!*

Longing for encouragement and praise takes energy better used in tending to the duties at hand.

Besides, other folks don't appreciate our challenges anyway. I saw that years ago when a relative and I drove to Kentucky to take my grandparents, Papa and Mama Farley, and my aunt Adah to Michigan for a visit. An eight-hour drive was ahead, so my grandmother had packed an enormous lunch basket, topped with a large bunch of bananas, and placed it next to her on the front seat. She positioned her cane against her leg and settled in for the trip.

Lengthy road construction and numerous detours forced us to take alternate routes on narrow stretches of asphalt through the beautiful Appalachian Mountains. At the top of one more detour, we discovered a rock slide had covered the road.

As I looked at the beautiful valley below us, the relative let the car idle as he got out to survey the situation. Just as he climbed onto the rock pile, perhaps to see if he could get his Buick over it, the car stalled and began to roll backward.

I was in the backseat, wedged between Aunt Adah and Papa, but it was up to me to reach the brake. In an instant, I threw myself over the seat, knocking the lunch basket to the floor as I scrambled to stomp on the brakes.

When I got the car stopped, it was already several feet beyond the asphalt. And beyond that was a five-hundred-foot drop into the ravine below.

It was up to me to reach the brake. In an instant, I threw myself over the seat, knocking the lunch basket to the floor.

With the car safely braked, I released my breath and tried to push my heart out of my throat and back down into its proper position. Finally, I looked at Mama Farley. Surely she had some praise for my quick action that had saved the four of us from severe injury, if not death.

But she merely glanced at me as she picked up the scattered lunch. Then she muttered, "You smashed the bananas."

So much for my need for appreciation. But I can't fault my grandmother. After all, she hadn't recognized the danger, so she couldn't appreciate my effort. And that's how it is with other folks who don't understand our single-parent challenges. So we continue tackling the day-to-day challenges, knowing we are saving ourselves and our children. And we smile!

Prayer: Father God, I'm weary. Weary of not being appreciated, not being encouraged, not being understood. Wow. That felt good to say! But even as I confess all that to you, I'm asking for your help. May I draw on your strength. May I not expect people to provide what only you can.

Thoughts to Ponder

1. Do you ever envy married women? Why or why not?
2. Have you ever rescued others who didn't see the potential danger? If so, what was the situation?

3. Which relatives or friends do you wish would appreciate your challenges?

Personal Ponderings

Day 6

The True Haven
Realistic Views

But I trust in your unfailing love; my heart rejoices in your salvation. Psalm 13:5

We read the magazine articles. We know protecting our emotional health should be high on our priority list. So if that is another ball we need to juggle, how are we supposed to accomplish this important task?

Well, for starters, we can take a deep breath and determine to avoid jealousy and envy. After all, jealousy just wastes precious energy. But even as I say that, I'm remembering a business meeting a while back. As we took our seats around the conference table, the boss answered a secretary's inquiry about his wife with a report about the luncheon she had given for several of the ladies from their church. The table was set with crystal and china while calming hymns played quietly in the background. Each woman had rushed into the house but had been quickly soothed by the setting. "She created a haven for them," he said casually.

Immediately, envy was my companion. Sure, his wife could provide a haven. She was a stay-at-home mother who had the luxury of concentrating on her adoring husband and children. Her days were her own. She could attend Bible study groups, shop at her convenience, bathe in the afternoon, and look nice for her husband, who paid the bills, talked to her, and helped her discipline their children. She wasn't juggling those duties and tensions all by herself. I confess I can't tell you one other thing that went on at the meeting.

> *"She created a haven for them," he said casually. Immediately, envy was my companion.*

Now when such situations occur, I remind myself I have chosen this lifestyle. True, I didn't choose to be single, but I did choose to raise my children alone, and I did choose to change careers in midlife to editing after having taught high school students for fifteen years.

Another get-tough attitude to adopt is to avoid hurtful fantasizing. Not all married women are like the woman who created a haven for her friends. Whenever I speak at church groups with women of varying ages and marital status, I always make a special point to acknowledge the single women, especially the single mothers. And I quote Isaiah 54:5—"For your Maker is your husband"—with my usual comment about our sharing the same husband. To my amazement—and sadness—I often have married women hug me afterward and whisper, "I wish I had *your* husband."

Yes, I understand the destructive power of envy and jealousy, but even though I've come a long way, I've still had moments of feeling very much alone. Our first Christmas in Colorado, Jay, Holly, and I attended an energetic musical with the thin plot of a family gathering in the Rocky Mountains for Christmas, singing joyful songs and expressing their love for each other. The show usually was given as part of a dinner package, so even our matinee audience was seated at large round tables. In the final moments before the curtain went up, waitresses hurried between the tables, delivering soft drinks.

When the program started, I was delighted by the high energy of the performers who sang and danced as though they were having a wonderful time. Then, during one particularly tender holiday song, I started to cry quietly as memories of past days rushed in. And, yes, I was lonesome even though Jay and Holly were sitting on either side of me. Just then the man across the table pulled his hand back toward his wife. My tears increased as I was convinced he was going to put his arm around her and give her shoulders a little squeeze. I envied his wife and decided he was a wonderful husband. My thoughts were moving faster than the man's arm.

> *To my amazement—and sadness—I often have married women hug me afterward and whisper, "I wish I had your husband."*

At last, with his hand all the way back, he reached for his soft drink instead of his wife!

I laughed aloud as another of life's realities shattered one more of my fantasies.

Prayer: Father God, I understand envy. Too often I look at what other women have and I want their situations. Help me remember that no one knows what goes on behind closed doors. May I be grateful for your presence in my life and find blessings in each new day.

Thoughts to Ponder

1. How do you react to the account of the boss who said his wife created a haven for her friends?
2. What specifics do you envy in the lives of others?
3. Have you ever envied another woman and later discovered her situation wasn't wonderful after all? If so, how did you feel?

Personal Ponderings

Day
7

What about Loneliness?

Who Will Bring Me Roses?

But just as he who called you is holy, so be holy in all you do; for it is written: "Be holy, because I am holy." 1 Peter 1:15–16

As I entered my second year of singlehood, well-meaning friends asked me when I'd get married again. I laughingly answered I wouldn't think about that until somebody showed up with a dozen roses. Then I changed the subject.

That evening as I mentally replayed the conversation, knowing I often veil the truth with my humor, I asked myself a tough question: Would I really be attracted to the first guy who handed me roses? As I admitted he at least would get my attention, I made an important decision: I would plant my own garden.

The next morning, I was at our local gardening shop loading my car trunk with rosebushes and bags of peat moss. For the next several months, I pruned and sprayed—and kept fresh roses throughout the house, quietly marveling at the satisfaction I gained from the bright, fragrant blooms.

Slowly I began to "plant my own garden" in other areas of my life as well, even taking steps toward a new career in editing and public speaking. If I had waited for someone else to bring me roses, and supposedly rescue me from my single state, I would have missed the incredible path my life has taken the past several years.

Hear me: This is not a soapbox speech for forever singleness. It's an encouragement for you to seek the Lord's direction rather than giving in to a desperate insistence for rescue. If you want to remarry and be part of a new family, go for it. But let the Lord heal you first rather than waiting for someone to show up with life's "roses."

Admittedly, I made a tough choice when I decided to put all thoughts of remarriage on hold for ten years. And although it is not the choice every single mother will—or should—make, I know it was the right one for me.

Why ten years? Well, the women in my family have a history of longevity, so I've often kidded I plan to live to be 102—and then die of smoke inhalation when my cake, with all the flaming candles, is brought in. And since I believe in the Old Testament concept of the tithe, I decided to tithe my very life. Thus, I chose ten years to learn more about the Lord and more about myself. After all, I had been Mitch's daughter, Don's wife, Jay and Holly's mother; I wanted to find Sandra Aldrich. And I did. Oh, she's feisty and has a tendency to shoot from the lip too much, but she's funny and strong and occasionally even wise. And I never would have found her if I'd thrown myself into another relationship in those early days of single parenting.

I genuinely believe my life never would have turned out this way if I had settled for what my extended family and even society expected instead of what God wanted to give me. And I believe God wanted to give me more of himself, not another husband.

I also was convinced the Lord was preparing me for another career, and I felt sure a second husband would just talk me into going back to teach in the high school classroom. Besides, I'd seen too many problems in second marriages. The divorce rate nationwide is 50 percent for first marriages, 70 to 80 percent for second marriages. I didn't want to be one of those statistics. So, recognizing that the mortality rate of second marriages is even higher than first marriages, I determined to save myself from getting into such a mess.

> *I genuinely believe my life never would have turned out this way if I had settled for what my extended family and even society expected instead of what God wanted to give me.*

Still, women in my Appalachian culture are expected to remarry, so I had to reason with aunts or cousins who made comments at every family gathering. To keep from saying what I was thinking, "That's none of your business," I'd mentally quote Proverbs 15:1—"A gentle answer turns away wrath, but a harsh word stirs up anger." But I still was irritated by the inquiries.

My friend Rose finally helped me break out of that anger trap when she said, "You're giving everyone too much credit when you think they *really* care about your decisions. They don't; they're too involved in their own problems."

I laughed, decided she was right, and promptly stopped worrying over the comments about remarriage. Amazingly, as I stopped arguing about my chosen status, the relatives gradually found more interesting topics to talk about.

A friend even said she admired the fact that I was *taking charge* of my life rather than merely *reacting* to everything. Then she leaned toward me. "But don't put God and his future for you in a little box."

I thought about that for several days and then prayed, "Lord, you know I want only what you want. But if I can have my druthers, I'd druther remain single.

> *"You're giving everyone too much credit when you think they* really *care about your decisions. They don't; they're too involved in their own problems."*

All I need are friends who will smile when I come into a room."

Now that I'm past that ten-year goal, do I regret my decision? Not for a minute.

Prayer: Father God, my status as a single mother is filled with more challenges and temptations than I ever dreamed. Help me draw from your strength. Help me concentrate on your presence and your guidance instead of giving in to fear. Help me find joy in each new day now as I prepare for the bright future you are planning.

Thoughts to Ponder

1. In what ways would you like to "plant your own garden" in your life? What steps do you need to take?
2. Do you have relatives and friends who try to plan your life? If so, how do you react?
3. How do you fight the temptations that surround you?

Personal Ponderings

Day
8

Roses with Thorns

Looking at the Past

Forgetting what is behind and straining toward what is ahead,
I press on toward the goal to win the prize for which God has
called me heavenward in Christ Jesus. Philippians 3:13–14

I'm glad I'd worked through various issues about dating and the
longing to be rescued the first year of my singlehood, because
one autumn morning I awakened with the biblical thought from
1 Peter 1:16, "Be holy." The idea was so compelling I started praying for strength to face whatever temptation was coming my way.

Deep in my gut, I knew my vow was about to be challenged.
I didn't have to wait long. A couple of weeks later, an old boyfriend—I'll call him Will—came back into my life. He had con-
tacted me shortly after my husband died, but I'd ignored his note.
Now he wrote again, signing off with the simple, "Friends do not
forget."

I didn't answer that note either, but I was consumed by it for weeks. I was finding single parenting much more difficult than I'd ever imagined. And I had not yet learned to be comfortable with the silence after Jay and Holly had gone to bed. More than once I paced the house after they were asleep, thankful Will and I had never been intimate to further complicate my emotions and glad he was several states away.

And now Will was saying softly into the phone, "Let me back into your life."

I stammered, "But I'm not the same person you knew. Besides, I've gained weight."

He chuckled. "You've gained a *lot* of weight. But that's never mattered to me. I've always thought you were terrific."

My thoughts bumped against each other. A man saying the extra pounds didn't matter? And how did he know what I looked like *now*? We hadn't talked since the day years earlier when he'd shaken hands with the one who would be my husband and told him to be good to me.

> *Will was saying softly into the phone, "Let me back into your life."*

Adding to my emotional upheaval was Will's account of the divorce from his alcoholic wife and that he too had struggled with a drinking problem. And, to hear him tell it, I was the cause of his bad choices. "I hit the bottle pretty bad after we broke up," he said into the phone.

We broke up? And all along, I'd been thinking *he* broke up with *me*. Obviously, we had been two naïve kids who needed to talk things through, yet had been without anybody to help us communicate.

Now that I'm on this side of the trauma, I'm shaking my head at all I put myself through back then. Those years were rough—I was experiencing confusing emotions over the way Will's life had turned out and over the false guilt I felt because of his decision to deal with disappointment through alcohol.

I knew I couldn't go back and undo Will's past pain, and I certainly didn't want Jay and Holly dealing with trauma that had been on the scene long before they were born. So there was nothing to do but lean even more on the Lord and trust him to bring his good out of my turmoil. And part of his good, I felt, would be in his ultimately using my experience to encourage another confused single mother also trying to wade through the decision of whether or not she could reconstruct her life with an old boyfriend.

> *Now that I'm on this side of the trauma, I'm shaking my head at all I put myself through back then.*

There! I've confessed I *do* understand your frustrations. But I trust you will listen to the Lord and not just to me. As you listen to him, he will guide you into the regret-free future he wants for you.

Prayer: Father God, yes, single parenting is more difficult than I had imagined. I know we are supposed to walk by faith, but each day offers another disappointment and another temptation. So I'm back to my usual plea: Help. Please help. Amazingly, as I asked for your help just now, I felt your presence and your strength. Thank you. Thank you.

Thoughts to Ponder

1. Does your past contain any "if onlys"?
2. What helps you process regrets from past years?
3. What goals have you set for a brighter future?

Personal Ponderings

A Morning Walk

Day
9

Heed the Warnings

> Now to him who is able to do immeasurably more than all
> we ask or imagine, according to his power that is at work
> within us. Ephesians 3:20

Several of my friends who sew or do needlework pour their
frustration into craft projects. So I did the same thing following my difficult but right decision not to allow Will, a former
boyfriend, back into my life. I bought a wall hanging onto which
I embroidered:

> Lord, I have a problem . . . it's me.
> Child, I have an answer . . . it's me.

Grammatically the sentences might not have been right, but
theologically they were perfect. As I embroidered bright green
leaves and orange flowers around the brown words, I breathed
a prayer into every stitch. Gradually, I was learning that once we

give something to the Lord, he usually takes care of it in ways we hadn't expected. As I worked on the wall hanging, he was working in me, creating a new woman.

Out of my pain over the way Will's marriage had been destroyed by alcohol, I had begun working with the late Jim Broome, cofounder of the Detroit-based Alcoholics for Christ. I'd written an article, "What Makes Alcoholics Stop," that summarized many of the principles Jim taught. Those two thousand words opened the way for the offer of an editorial position with a New York Christian magazine. I promptly accepted—and started a new career that never would have opened if I'd settled for less than what the Lord had planned.

The Scripture for today's devotion is Ephesians 3:20, which says, "Now to him who is able to do immeasurably more than all we ask or imagine, according to his power that is at work within us." I don't know about you, but I can imagine all sorts of wonderful things, so I'm awed by his promise to do more for us than even what our minds can conceive. He did that for me, though, and I'm convinced he will do that for you. Sure, maybe you won't be asked to accept a midlife career change and move eight hundred miles away. But the Lord enjoys giving his children gifts, so who knows what adventures are ahead for you if you will trust him and wait for his gift. This is where trust comes in as we wait for him to open doors instead of giving in to panic and settling for less than his best.

As I speak around the country, I'm saddened by the number of women who tell me stories that begin with "I wish" and "If only." Too often they've rushed into and even stayed in sad situations because of loneliness. What an awful trap! And the entire time, they keep telling themselves things will get better. Yet they never do.

I think of Millie, who was convinced she wasn't whole unless she was half of a couple. So after her divorce, she latched on to the first man who looked her way. What she refused to see, though, was his rude attitude toward her. In her loneliness, she tried to believe he was the answer to her problems and that their relationship would get better as time went on. I don't have to tell you her heart was broken again, and she wound up feeling used.

Years ago, when we still lived in Michigan, I learned that the wrong kind of perseverance doesn't guarantee good outcomes. One beautiful autumn morning, I had the day off from work and had driven Jay and Holly to school. Because it was such a nice day, I decided to leave the car in the lot and walk the three miles back home. I'd walk back in the afternoon and drive us all home. All I had to do was stroll down the school drive to Joy Road, turn right onto Lilly Road, and head home.

> *The entire time, they keep telling themselves things will get better. Yet they never do.*

But I looked across the grassy field to my right. Hmm. If I went that way, I'd get onto Lilly Road that much quicker, with only wet shoes from the dewy grass.

So I started off through the field, glorying in the beautiful morning. Soon my shoes and socks, indeed, were wet. The grass was deeper than I had thought, but it surely wouldn't get any deeper, or so I told myself. I'd keep going. After a few more feet, however, I realized the field had a gentle downhill slope to it. The grass that had looked only ankle deep from the parking lot was now up to my knees.

I paused, looking carefully at the several yards of grass I still had to wade through before I could be on the other side of the field. *Well, it can't get any worse,* I thought. *My shoes, socks, and slacks are already drenched. Might as well keep going.* In less than a dozen steps, however, the ground seemed to disappear, and the grass was over my head! I slogged through the ravine, feeling as though I was fighting my way through the jungle in some B movie.

But I'd gone too far now to go back. The worst was over. A few more steps, and I'd be at the edge of the field and on Lilly

Road. By now I was drenched from head to toe with the heavy dew. But, sure enough, as I plunged ahead, the grass was getting shorter again. It was at my waist, my knees, and finally just over my shoes. I was free!

But my rejoicing was short-lived. Just ahead was a deep, mud-filled gully. I stood there for several moments, looking at the muddy slope on the far side that would be impossible to climb up, even if I could safely get down this side.

In a moment of wild Tarzan fantasy, I even surveyed the large tree nearby, looking for a vine on which I could swing over to the other side. Nothing.

I looked back at the grassy field through which I had just come. I didn't want to claw my way through that again. *Surely I can climb this tree some way and drop over to the other side,* I thought. *No, they'll never find my body before spring.* I could do nothing now but turn around and go all the way back through that scary, wet grass. I drove home then, but in much worse shape than if I'd taken the longer, safer way in the first place.

> *My rejoicing was short-lived. Just ahead was a deep, mud-filled gully.*

But some good came out of that experience: Now when I'm tempted to take the easy way out of a situation, I give it another long, hard look first. That invariably takes care of the temptation. And the miserable results that could follow.

Prayer: Father God, I understand the "But it can't get any worse" scenario. Help me not panic and, thus, choose the way that looks easy but is filled with heartbreak. Help me seek your way. Help me trust you for a bright future. In other words, "Help!"

Thoughts to Ponder

1. What temptations have you faced? How did you handle each one?
2. Have you ever continued on a difficult path, convinced it couldn't get worse? What happened?
3. As you examine the future in light of Ephesians 3:20, what are you asking the Lord to do?

Personal Ponderings

Embracing the Abundant Life

Don't Just Settle

The thief comes only to steal and kill and destroy; I have come that they may have life, and have it to the full. John 10:10

Believe me, I'm not against remarriage. I'm just asking that you not rush to fill the void and not look for rescue. I still remember the Michigan woman who told me, "Keep telling

47

women to pray a lot before they jump into a new relationship. Everything I went through as a single mother was a piece of cake compared to trying to blend two families."

Dr. John Canine, a Detroit-area therapist, is often asked when it's time to start dating again after a heartbreak. He offers the "three Cs" as guidelines: companionship, common interests, and commitment.

People need one another, so dating fills the need for someone to talk to, to enjoy events with, to share memories with. But all too often folks jump from companionship to commitment, skipping the important step of common interest.

If the Lord has someone waiting for you, he most likely *won't* send him to ring your doorbell, hand you a dozen roses, and say, "Hi, I'm from the Lord."

So it's okay to let your friends know you're ready to date again. Everyone seems to have at least one "wonderful guy" for you on their Christmas list. And who knows? He may *really* be as nice as they say. Just don't rush. And don't skip the common interest connection, including the all-important shared faith part.

You may have to initiate a few meetings too. But bypass the local dances and secular singles clubs. If you want to meet a godly man, look in the places where godly people gather. Start by taking part in your church spring clean-ups, joining the mission committee, or teaching Sunday school. But be careful here too. At a Florida singles' conference, I was encouraging my audience to take part in church activities when a man interrupted me. He then described how guys know church women are sexually clean. So they attend services just long enough to scout out the territory for a lonely woman and pick up the correct theology phrases that will win her heart—and body. Then he softly added, "I know what I'm talking about. I used to be one of those guys." My jaw dropped at the new information my audience and I had just gained.

If you're not sure you're ready to plunge headlong into the dating scene, you can test the waters by talking to men in casual settings. It's amazing how much you can learn about their general philosophies just by asking a simple question in a Sunday school class.

I remember the morning someone used the phrase "normal family," and I innocently asked for a definition. The guy three seats over jumped into a tirade ranging from blasting working mothers to condemning Christian counselors. I never got my definition, but I certainly had more than enough information about him.

If you're not sure you're ready to plunge headlong into the dating scene, you can test the waters by talking to men in casual settings.

Set your standards, then firmly stick to them. In Margo's freshman high school health class, they had a unit on dating. One of the questions was, "Should you kiss on a first date?" to get the students to think *before* the date and, thereby, set limits.

Maybe we need to reapply some of that same mentality to our present adult relationships. If you're thinking about dating, do you know what you want in a man? Or will just any warm, breathing creature do? So draw up your list, my friend, but give it some heavy-duty thought and prayer first. And God bless you on your reentry into the dating scene.

Before some friends decided I was hopeless, they asked if I was "seeing" anybody yet. I usually answered with a quick, "I don't have room either in my closets or in my life for a man!"

But those who were closest to me would persist, might even clear their throats and then ask, "But what about your . . . uh . . . *needs?*"

I'd answer, "I try not to think about them," and promptly change the subject.

After I had struggled with this I heard a quotation from Edward K. Longabaugh, a former Colorado Springs pastor, that I wish I'd heard earlier to help me verbalize my goal: "Sometimes our needs need to take a backseat to the needs of others—not out of weakness but out of the strength Christ has given us."

> *"Sometimes our needs need to take a backseat to the needs of others—not out of weakness but out of the strength Christ has given us."*

And, for me, those others were my children.

So what *are* singles supposed to do? Various authors have differing ideas, but most agree the only activity that really works is *sublimation*. Rechanneling sexual energy into our work, sports, or other wholesome activities results in creative productivity.

In case you're thinking, "Oh, yeah, sure," let me assure you from personal experience it *is* possible to live a fulfilled life without a physical relationship. How?

- By staying out of inappropriate situations. (You know what they are!)
- By not watching movies that will stir up old longings.
- By not reading inappropriate material.
- By working hard and going to bed tired.
- By pouring energy into other activities.

When we make these efforts, we can smile at ourselves in the mirror and remain genuinely fulfilled.

A few months into my singlehood, I awakened early one Saturday and couldn't get back to sleep as I remembered leisurely weekend mornings when I was married. Determined to think of other things, I asked myself what I'd really like to do over the school break. The most amazing thought bubbled up: visit an Old Order Amish family! With my own farm background, I admire the Amish work habits and preservation of the old ways. So I called an Indiana friend who worked with several Amish. Within the next few weeks, my children and I were invited into an Amish home belonging to John and Katherine.

All their children and grandchildren arrived to greet us. The men were dressed in dark blue trousers and white shirts and took off their flat straw hats as they entered the house. The women wore dark blue or brown dresses and took off their large bonnets to reveal smaller, white caps covering their bound hair.

Even though I had dressed in a navy blue skirt and white blouse out of respect for their simple ways, I still felt overdressed, especially as those beautiful, silent children stared at my watch.

The family patriarch, John, politely asked about my work, and I told about what I did for a living. But I made sure I included details of my own Kentucky farm background, adding stories about some zany neighbors. John laughed along with the others and gave his blessing for future visits.

> *Rechanneling sexual energy into our work, sports, or other wholesome activities results in creative productivity.*

Over the next few years, my children and I graciously were welcomed into Amish homes. The high point of one visit came when the matriarch of that first home, Katherine, insisted we stay for the Sunday supper. Twenty-five of us were seated at one wide table filled with hearty dishes I remembered from my own farm days. As I buttered a wheat muffin, I marveled at the Saturday morning sublimation that had resulted in this wonderful friendship. And none of that would have happened if I'd chosen the world's way of releasing tension.

Prayer: Father God, I really need your help in this area. I'm intrigued that rechanneling my sexual energy into so-called wholesome activities will result in creative productivity. I don't understand that, but I'm willing to try.

Thoughts to Ponder

1. What do you think about Dr. Canine's dating guidelines: companionship, common interests, and commitment?
2. Have you learned more than you expected about a person just through his or her reaction to a simple question? If so, what was the situation?
3. Sandra chose a visit to the Amish in answer to her own question about what she'd like to do. What adventure would you choose?

Personal Ponderings

_____

_____

_____

Day 11

With Open Eyes
Be Forewarned but Not Afraid

Look to the LORD and his strength; seek his face always.
Psalm 105:4

When I was in my twenties, I thought women twice my age and older were beyond being interested in physical relationships. Well, I'm that advanced age now, and I've discovered even a tired-looking body and wrinkles don't mean the hormones are tired and wrinkled too. Those little critters are ageless.

But no matter what the movies present, the world is filled with countless numbers of us who have learned we *can* control hormonal urgings with the same ability we control anger. And if we also are wise, we'll discern the difference between the man who's interested in a serious, ongoing relationship and the guy who's on the prowl for a one-night stand.

In my files, I have an undated clipping from the *Reporter Dispatch* newspaper of Mount Kisco, New York. It says, "Men tend to misinterpret female friendliness as a sexual come-on, according to research by psychologist Frank Saal"—then at Kansas State University. In one study, Saal had two hundred students respond to a video of a female student asking a male professor for an extension on her paper. Women saw the exchange simply as a friendly exchange. Men saw the same scene but perceived the student was being flirty. Saal concluded, "Men tend to over-sexualize what women say and do."

Because I'm naturally outgoing, this matter of how one's speech and actions are interpreted is an area I have to watch. I'm fascinated by people and love talking to them, telling them my outlandish stories, and laughing at theirs. And I'm so thrilled with the joy of this moment—one of the silver linings left over from the School of Hard Knocks—that my friendliness can be misinterpreted. I discovered the sad truth when a fellow teacher asked me out.

He was married but a known womanizer, so I was devastated by his thinking I was *that* type. I tell myself that if he asked *now*, I'd let him know how wrong his invitation was. But back then, I merely said I didn't think it would be a good idea, closed the door to my empty classroom, and sobbed at the new world singlehood had thrust me into.

That was the first but not the last unwanted, uninvited proposition I received from a professional peer. After I left teaching and became a writer and editor, I worked on freelance projects, wrote scripts for videos, accepted special assignments from numerous organizations, and worked with various photographers and artists. I treat everyone the same, and I don't go looking for signs someone is flirting with me. Since I'm so outgoing, I didn't read the signs that a longtime friend and colleague in Michigan was starting to make a move.

He'd kidded me about being lonesome, and I wish I'd said right then, "We've just crossed into inappropriate territory. Let's change the subject, shall we?"

Instead, I thought he was being big brotherly. Stupid me! He'd even made little innuendos, going beyond typical teasing, and was unkind to his wife in my presence.

Then one day while we were working on a project, we stopped for lunch. Little bells were going off in my head, but I thought I was safe. After all, this was a longtime friend. Besides, I assumed my weight was my protection; I was sure I wasn't going to have any of the come-on problems all those gorgeous, slim single moms had. Wrong!

> *I was sure I wasn't going to have any of the come-on problems all those gorgeous, slim single moms had. Wrong!*

We had other stops to make, so as we left the restaurant, I asked, "Where to now?"

He smiled. "Well, we could always go back to your place and have a torrid love affair."

I was stunned but managed to say sternly, "I already have enough trouble in my life."

He laughed and changed the subject to details of our project. However, I wasn't hearing one thing he said. Instead, I rehashed what I *wish* I'd said—all the way from, "I'm disappointed in you for making such a suggestion," to, "Come really close so I can hit you really hard!" If I had challenged him, though, he undoubtedly would have insisted he was joking and maybe even accused me of not having a sense of humor. But some things are not joking matters.

Yet I couldn't react the way I wanted to because I kept thinking the whole situation must have been my fault or he wouldn't have said anything so outrageous. I know better now.

Since those encounters, I've discovered my introduction to the world of womanizers was mild. My friends tell me horror stories of men cooing into the phone, "My wife's visiting her mother. I bet you're lonely too. Why don't I come over and we can—uh—talk."

Sadly, enough guys meet with enough success in these approaches that they think *all* single women can be won over sooner or later. The only way we single women are going to get men to treat us with respect is to demand it with our own high standards. So let's keep looking to the Lord for his guidance. May we let his strength become ours.

> *Yet I couldn't react the way I wanted to because I kept thinking the whole situation must have been my fault or he wouldn't have said anything so outrageous.*

Prayer: *Father God, help me see the truth in each situation I encounter. And help me respond appropriately and in your strength.*

Thoughts to Ponder

1. What's your reaction to the study psychologist Frank Saal performed at Kansas State University, which showed the

different perceptions men and women had of the same scene?

2. Have you received unwelcome advances? If so, how did you respond?

3. What suggestions do you have for women who encounter unwelcome advances?

Personal Ponderings

Day 12

Sweet Fantasy

Bitter Regrets

So do not fear, for I am with you; do not be dismayed, for I am your God. I will strengthen you and help you. I will uphold you with my righteous right hand. Isaiah 41:10

We single women talk about the unsavory characters we've met, but what about those times when we're attracted not to the womanizer but to someone wonderful—the pastor, a coworker, or a neighbor?

That emotion has a name: transference. All the energy and attention that went into the previous relationship has to go somewhere, and sometimes it's directed toward someone who is not an appropriate recipient.

Misunderstood transference can tempt lonely people into inappropriate situations that can lead even to adultery. And the path to regret usually starts with an emotional longing that turns into a physical action. Too often we hear of a pastor counseling a distraught woman and then having an affair with her, further complicating her life and destroying his ministry.

Unfortunately, that very scenario happened with three of my friends. When I heard the news, I was devastated, because previously each one had my utmost respect.

One man had an ill wife and started meeting with a mutual friend to pray for his bride. That friend was a tired, underappreciated young wife who looked forward to their prayer meetings. Soon they were no longer praying but still meeting, and the church rocked with the scandal.

Another woman worked on a ministry project with a staff member of a large church. They'd been friends for years and hadn't planned for anything to happen, but it did. He lost his position in the church, she lost her husband's respect, and both would give anything for the affair not to have happened.

Another friend was the office counselor type, and he wanted to help a coworker who was having problems with her ex-husband. It started with kind words, progressed to lunches, and culminated in an affair that threatened his marriage and cost him ministry leadership and community respect.

Yes, even godly people can develop intense and inappropriate feelings for someone. But if you find yourself fantasizing, don't signal it to the other person. If you keep your active imagination to yourself and ask the Lord to help you conquer it, then you are the only one involved. But as soon as you signal your passion to the other person, your intimate thoughts may ignite a fire that will destroy marriages and lives in ways you never dreamed and, I trust, never wanted.

But remember that others can misread even our innocent intentions. I remember the moment I was suddenly and sharply reminded of another hazard of being a single mother: being perceived as a threat to marital happiness.

The wife of a colleague let me know in no uncertain terms she didn't want me working on a project with her husband. She didn't like the way it looked. Actually, she meant she didn't like the way it looked to *her*. Her words momentarily left me stunned and speechless. Limp with disbelief at her implication, I sank back into my chair and stared out the window at the beautiful lawn beyond. I may have appeared to be sitting calmly, but I was mentally clawing the air as her words catapulted me into the role of an imaginary would-be home wrecker. Yet I'm not angry with this concerned wife. Actually, she did me a favor. No longer was I "Don Aldrich's widow" but "Sandra Aldrich—single woman."

> *If you keep your active imagination to yourself and ask the Lord to help you conquer it, then you are the only one involved.*

And for that reminder, I'll always be grateful.

Okay, okay, you may be thinking. *So get back to the dating again part.*

Once I'd moved past the temptation over Will, the former boyfriend, the rest of the ten years governed by my vow sped by with all the fun and crises of single parenting. Suddenly, both kiddos were in college, so I accepted a coffee date with someone I'd known since fourth grade. And, yes, I was a nervous wreck deciding what to wear and reminding my independent self to wait for traditional him to open the car door.

Since that coffee outing, I occasionally accept dinner invitations or enjoy an afternoon of exploring local antique shops. But I've found the dating scene to have changed too much in the years I've stayed away. Besides, as I speak around the country, I hear too many horror stories from women who are facing intense sexual pressure after only a few dates. And, in case you're wondering, I've remained celibate all these years. Not only don't I have time for the dating and courtship routine, but at my age, the guys who whistle at me are in their late seventies and eighties. And somehow when they blow out their teeth along with the wolf whistle, any romantic effect is lost. Besides, one of the men from church looked at me adoringly over dinner and flat out let me know he's looking for a good woman to cook and clean! I should have given him the name of my cleaning lady, but instead I said, "Honey, I write books; I don't dust knick-knacks."

I was mentally clawing the air as her words catapulted me into the role of an imaginary would-be home wrecker.

Do I regret my lost opportunity? Not at all. My life is too full now to add one more item to my juggling act. Okay, okay, you may remind me of this when you hear I've run away with some banjo-playing mountain man.

Prayer: Father God, thank you for your promise to be with me in all situations. You know my thoughts and my temptations, so help me talk to you honestly about them and then draw strength from you.

Thoughts to Ponder

1. What examples of transference have you witnessed—or experienced? What happened?

2. What decisions have you made about dating?

3. How would you have answered the man who announced he was looking for a good woman to cook and clean?

Personal Ponderings

_____

_____

_____

<table>
<tr><td>Day
13</td><td></td></tr>
</table>

Guilt—An Unwelcome Companion

But Not the Victor

If we confess our sins, he is faithful and just and will forgive us our sins and purify us from all unrighteousness. 1 John 1:9

Guilt and I are old acquaintances. Why? Because, like you, I'm a single mother and I had to work while my children were young. In fact, I still have to work.

But years ago, whenever I felt guilty about not being home for my children, I'd remind myself about a Kentucky widow. Her husband had been injured in the mine—strained his heart after pushing a runaway coal cart aside, she told me, and died a couple of years later.

She had no choice but to go to work as a hired girl and turn her two- and four-year-old daughters over to her parents. She saw them only once a month for several years.

Like her, most of us don't have a choice either. We have to work.

And with everything else we're juggling, we don't need to lay extra guilt on ourselves. Others will do that for us quite readily. So let's just accept the fact that some things are the way they have to be and grab any extra moment we can muster for ourselves and our children.

> *Over the years, I've learned guilt comes in three forms: true, misplaced, and false.*

I used to think guilt came in only one flavor—the plain ol' vanilla type that told me I never could do enough for my children. But over the years, I've learned guilt comes in three forms: true, misplaced, and false.

True guilt appears when we've done something wrong and need to ask forgiveness. You know—as when we've accused our child of misbehavior before we have the entire story.

Misplaced guilt occurs when we blame ourselves for something someone else did. For example, a twelve-year-old enjoys riding his bike to soccer practice after school. His mother doesn't think much about it—until he gets hit by a car. Then as she sits by his hospital bed, she thinks this wouldn't have happened if she'd been home, and that it's all her fault. No, it's the fault of the idiot who drove right past the stop sign.

False guilt often can be identified by the words *should* and *ought*. As in, "I should go all out for Christmas to make up for what my children have lost. I'll worry about the bills later." Or, "I ought to do all the housework myself since my children have enough challenges in life."

False guilt is what many of us deal with the most. And it's mean stuff.

I remember one winter afternoon in New York when our company closed early because of an impending storm. I arrived home thirty minutes before Jay and Holly's school bus, and I quickly stirred up a batch of chocolate chip cookies.

I'll never forget the look of surprise on my teens' faces when they opened the door and discovered I was there to greet them. They had barely shaken the snow off their coats when I exclaimed, "And I made cookies! I'm a mom again!"

I was so tormented that the sitter, not I, would witness his first-step milestone that I started to pray about it daily.

Even now, that is one of our family jokes. Obviously, I was trying to fit someone else's idea of what good mothers are supposed to do. But as single moms, we can't juggle our responsibilities if we let others heap guilt around our already stooped shoulders.

Sadly, some folks seem to enjoy throwing guilt our way. I went back to teaching when Jay was less than a year old. One of the women with whom I worked in the church nursery repeatedly said, "You're going to miss his first steps."

As Jay's first birthday approached, he began to pull himself up and then work his way across a room by clutching furniture and walls. I was so tormented that the sitter, not I, would witness his first-step milestone that I started to pray about it daily. Somewhere during my prayers, the thought came that even if I missed the first steps, there'd be plenty of other firsts to rejoice in.

Then late one afternoon, while I was preparing dinner, little Jay worked his way around the kitchen. Suddenly he giggled, let go of the wall, and took three big steps right into my open arms.

The following Sunday at church, I had just put on my nursery apron when my coworker stormed in. "I can't believe it!" she snarled. "We went to my cousin's wedding last night and left Becky with a sitter for the first time. And she took her first steps while we were gone."

Amazingly, I felt no glee that what she had assumed for me had befallen her. But I do remember.

So how should we handle guilt? This is when I like to recall the AA motto: Let go and let God. In other words, we need to invite God into every situation, every concern, every need. Yes, it takes effort to whisper a prayerful "Help" when we're feeling overwhelmed or anxious. And too often we are so focused on guilt's weight that we refuse to ask for God's help, perhaps because we think we don't deserve it.

At the top of this devotion, I quoted 1 John 1:9: "If we confess our sins, he is faithful and just and will forgive us our sins and purify us from all unrighteousness." So if our almighty, perfect heavenly Father wants to set us free through his forgiveness, how can we refuse that gift?

Yes, all of us have situations we wish we'd handled differently. Maybe we can't undo those times, but we can learn from them. So when we are wrong, let's confess it to the Lord, draw on his strength, ask forgiveness of the person we've hurt, and take our new wisdom into future events. Guilt does not have to be our constant companion.

Prayer: Father God, I'm tired. Tired of feeling as though I'm failing my children. Tired of other people telling me what I should do. Tired of feeling guilty at every turn. So help. Please help.

Thoughts to Ponder

1. Do you ever struggle with guilt? If so, over what issues?
2. Do you find it helpful to know guilt comes in three forms—true, misplaced, and false?

3. How do you respond to those who try to heap guilt on you? How would you like to respond?

Personal Ponderings

Day 14

Guilt and the Normal Mom

Juggling Work and More

Do not be anxious about anything, but in every situation, by prayer and petition, with thanksgiving, present your requests to God. Philippians 4:6

Jay and Holly quickly figured out I can handle a crisis but I can't handle guilt. Not only did they use that fact whenever it was to their advantage, but that's how we got Petey—the tiger cat who took over our household.

For months, they had been asking for a pet, especially because they remembered our previous animals. At first, I patiently explained our schedule, saying it wouldn't be fair to an animal to be left alone so much.

They'd countered with the thought that a cat likes being left alone. I again said no.

They described the new litter of kittens in the neighborhood, adding they'd be "put to sleep" if a home wasn't found soon. I remained unmoved.

Finally, Holly looked at me with sorrowful eyes. "How come when we ask you for a kitty, you always say no, but the *first* time we asked Daddy, he said yes!"

I knew I'd lost. "Go get your cat, Holly."

Both kiddos were out the door almost before I finished the sentence.

Sadly, that wasn't the only time guilt directed my decisions. And I especially understand the guilt the working mother carries—caused by the amount of time she (we!) must spend away from the children while earning the daily bread. But instead of bemoaning our fate, allow me to offer a solution: flextime. By offering flextime schedules to those who want them, employers will help lessen our guilt and, at the same time, benefit themselves by gaining an employee with greatly improved morale.

Let us women take care of what's important to us, and we'll also take care of what's important to our bosses.

A recent award-winning movie had a riveting scene in which a slave begged her new owner to buy her two children as well. As the woman pleaded to keep her little ones, she said she'd be the best slave he'd ever have if he wouldn't separate them. He refused and bought only her.

As our audience sighed or shed tears at the scene, we knew the owner had made a mistake. The woman's grief was so deep, she couldn't work. The slave owner had ignored a basic principle today's managers need to understand too: Let us women take care of what's important to us, and we'll also take care of what's important to our bosses.

When we moved to New York, my work schedule thrust Jay and Holly into the world of latchkey kids. I wasn't handling the routine well, so I talked it over with my boss. He let me start work earlier so I could arrive home only an hour later than my children. Not only did that help my situation, but the business actually got extra hours out of me since I often worked through lunch.

> *Like it or not, Christian women are working outside the home, and Christian organizations especially should offer flexible hours whenever possible for those who need them.*

Like it or not, Christian women *are* working outside the home, and Christian organizations especially should offer flexible hours whenever possible for those who need them. I'm not looking forward to standing before the Lord to give an account for my parenting. But I hope I get to ask that several bosses be made to stand there with me.

Most of us get tired just from juggling guilt; we don't need to add worry. Thus, safe and affordable child care is of utmost importance and goes a long way toward alleviating a working mother's worry. If your work site doesn't have a preschool nursery, pray a lot and look at what is available in your area. Here are a few suggestions worth checking:

- Does a nearby church have a child care program?
- Do you have relatives who would enjoy watching your children while getting paid?
- Is a mother staying home with her kids willing to look after one or two more for a monthly fee?

- Could the directors of senior citizens clubs and organizations in your area suggest responsible and energetic retirees who could use extra income and would enjoy contact with youngsters?
- Can you find college students who enjoy kids and can use some extra income?

No matter what solution you choose, check the references. Then once you've chosen the caregiver, watch your child's demeanor when in that person's presence. Don't ignore any sign of fear. The child's safety tops convenience.

Speaking of safety, here are a few ways we can ensure our older children are safe at home when we're not there:

- Make sure your children know whom to call in an emergency.
- Stress that they are never to open the door and are never to tell a stranger on the phone they're alone.

I always instructed Jay and Holly to say, "I'm sorry, but my mother can't come to the phone right now. If you'll leave a message, I'll have her call you back shortly." One of the men with whom I taught was angry at lunch, saying he'd called the night before but Holly wouldn't let him talk to me.

Most of us get tired just from juggling guilt; we don't need to add worry.

"You couldn't have been in the shower that long!" he snarled, guessing at the reason for Holly's deliberately vague explanation on the phone.

"Oh, so you're the one who wouldn't leave his name," I said. And then, though I was under no obligation, I explained, "I was at the grocery store."

"Well, she could have told me you weren't home."

"Why? She doesn't know you."

"Well, that's dumb."

The other mothers at the lunch table chimed in immediately, coming to my defense and letting him know he really was out of line.

It's also important to address your children's concerns.

- Ask them what they dislike most about being home alone and then work out ways to make that area less painful. A friend's son, Jamie, dreaded coming into a dark house in the winter. His mother's simple investment in an electric timer took care of the problem.

- Make sure your kids have both your work phone number and, if you have one, your cell phone number. But insist they don't call you to referee their squabbles.

Sharon, a recent single mom, remembers a tired mother in a fabric department who got a call right in the middle of cutting a length of material. Sharon could hear her pleading with first one son and then another, saying she'd help them settle it when she got home in a couple of hours.

Sharon confesses her first thought was to wonder why the woman didn't stay home with her kids, "where she belonged." It was easy for Sharon to be self-righteous. Her physician husband paid her bills; their children were cared for a few hours each day by a housekeeper. But when her husband left her for his nurse, Sharon's world came tumbling down. Eventually, she even had to take a job outside the home. Then she remembered the woman from the fabric department with a new understanding.

Prayer: Father God, this isn't the life I dreamed about. But here I am—facing challenge after challenge. So I welcome your invitation to present all my requests and concerns directly to you. But you'll have to help me do that with a good attitude. I confess I'd rather just whine.

Thoughts to Ponder

1. Have your children ever used guilt to change your mind? If so, what happened?
2. Would flextime work for your schedule? Have you presented this idea to your boss? If so, what happened? If not, what are your concerns about doing that?
3. How do you make sure your children are safe—whether in the care of someone else or when you aren't home?

Personal Ponderings

Day
15

Guilt and Long Summers

Prayer and Creativity

If any of you lacks wisdom, [she] should ask God, who gives generously to all without finding fault, and it will be given to [her]. James 1:5

Summertime, and the worry is heavy. Yes, summer is an especially tough time for us single moms who work outside the home, especially if our children are too old for babysitters but too young for jobs. Jay and Holly were in their early teens when we moved from the Detroit area to New York. Several years before, when we were a two-salary family, we had purchased a secondhand trailer at a lakeside Bible camp in Michigan. So I sent my young teens back there our first summer in New York and arranged for various relatives to take turns staying with them. I thought it was a perfect solution: My teens were with friends, and the responsible adults staying with them could enjoy the beach. I flew or drove out several times during those ten weeks.

Sounds perfect, huh? But, alas, the venture was doomed from the start. Several of the women in our lake neighborhood, who were married to businessmen and did not work outside the home, let me know I was robbing my teens. One of the kindest comments was, "I think it's terrible you won't be with your children."

At the end of the season, I sold the place—to free myself not only from the financial burden but also from trying to please forty other mothers.

The following summer, I enrolled Jay and Holly in several local day camps. When those ended, I signed them up for four weeks at an inexpensive Christian camp in northern New York.

I was surprised—and intrigued—at their personality dynamics while they were there. Both kids were given the same four-week sentence, but they handled it differently.

Holly was convinced from Day One she wouldn't survive those twenty-eight days. She looked longingly toward home and plotted how she could convince me to release her. The first postcard I received from her was addressed to "Four Weeks Aldrich." Her subtle humor delighted me, but I was determined she was going to stick it out.

Next, she shrewdly decided to write lengthy accounts to me of the campers spraying their sleeping bags every night to keep the crawling bugs away. Sigh. I let her come home, then, after a two-week sentencing: "The longest jail term ever, Mom!"

Meanwhile, Jay looked around and said, "Okay, I'm here for four weeks. What can I do to make it tolerable?"

After I made arrangements to rescue Holly from the crawling things, I told Jay he could come home at the same time.

"No, I'm not going to wimp out," he said.

I stressed it was okay to come home.

"No, I don't want you thinking I'm a wimp like Holly."

"Jay, I won't!"

"Mom, I don't want to see it in your eyes. Just don't do this to me next year."

I didn't.

> *She shrewdly decided to write lengthy accounts to me of the campers spraying their sleeping bags every night to keep the crawling bugs away.*

The next year, they spent time with relatives back in Michigan. The year after that, they both were old enough and responsible enough to have day jobs at the local shopping mall. Whew!

I confess I'm glad to be past that exhausting time. But if you're still there, pray a lot, talk to other single moms, look into church camps or the YMCA day camps. And always talk over the situation with trusted relatives, dear friends, and your youngsters. These days of summer don't have to sabotage your parenting.

Several of the single mothers in my present neighborhood are fortunate enough to have extended family willing to take their children for the summer. Tyler spends his vacations on his grandparents' Kentucky farm, Martin enjoys staying with his uncle and aunt in western Colorado. Perhaps you don't have to worry about summer child care because your children spend those months with their dad. But not everyone has relatives who can help for weeks at a time. That's why it's important to start planning long before summer arrives.

So take a deep breath, ask for the Lord's help, and don't despair. Whenever we think our situation is greater than our resources, we set ourselves up for more guilt. And I'm convinced such guilt can keep us trapped and defeated. Oh, how the Enemy loves to have us beat ourselves emotionally and concentrate on our failings instead of on the Lord's power.

> *Take a deep breath, ask for the Lord's help, and don't despair.*

Even though I've worked on a professional counseling team, my mother offers the best advice when it comes to dealing with guilt: "It's like plowing new ground. You can get hung up on a stump root and keep worrying at it all day, or you can pick up your plow and go on."

So pick up your plow! Solutions *are* available, and they will be revealed as you ask the Lord for his direction.

Prayer: Father God, please help me not to listen to judgmental comments about my summer plans for my children when I'm doing the best I can. And if I need to make changes, please show your solution.

Thoughts to Ponder

1. What summer challenges do you face?
2. How do you provide care for your children when they are out of school but you must work?
3. What summer solutions haven't worked for your family? Which ones have?

Personal Ponderings

Day 16	# Forgiving Others *An Important Decision*

> For if you forgive [others] when they sin against you, your heavenly Father will also forgive you. But if you do not forgive others their sins, your Father will not forgive your sins. Matthew 6: 14

One of the biggest doorways to emotional peace comes when we forgive those who have hurt us. Yes, I know we'd rather see them punished—maybe even in horrible ways. After all, we want them to hurt as much as we do. But what does that accomplish? Does it undo their wrong? Does it really bring us peace? No. So let's take a deep breath and think about forgiving them.

We've read the books and, better yet, the Scriptures about forgiveness, but following through still can be difficult. However, I'm convinced personal emotional freedom comes as we work through the situation to where we truly can forgive. I've lost count of the times I've reminded an angry woman that by holding a grudge she's hurting only herself, not the other person. I've even said, "He's not losing sleep over this; you are. You've got to let this go for your own sake." And letting go doesn't mean we say, "Hey, it's okay you were rotten to me. No problem. Really." Forgiveness is a process we must work through.

One of my Denver friends, Dr. Linda Williams, offered the best forgiveness advice I've ever received: "Forgiveness is the willingness to live with the consequences of another's sin." I like that. Often that choice to live with another's wrong actions allows us to get on with life.

> *Even as many of us mouth forgiveness outwardly, we're really seething inside.*

But what if that person doesn't acknowledge he or she hurt us or, worse yet, hurt our child? I'm well aware Jesus said in Matthew 5:39 and Luke 6:29 that if we get hit on one cheek, we're to turn the other as well. Yet, even as many of us mouth forgiveness outwardly, we're really seething inside. I fell into that trap a few years ago and had to learn the hard way that it's far better to talk over the situation immediately and not let it get lost in time.

A New York friend was aggravated with me, and when my daughter, Holly, stopped by her house, the woman said, "What are you doing here?" and shut the door in her face. Holly stood on the porch, bewildered at this uncharacteristic action on my friend's part. The woman opened the door again and said, "Are you still here?" and shut it again. Then she opened the door a third time and said, "I was just kidding. Come in."

Holly's visit was short. At dinner, she cried as she described the scene to her brother and me. I wish I had picked up the phone right then and asked for an explanation, but I thought my friend would see that as pettiness on my part. So I forced myself to talk about forgiveness with my teens. They accepted my so-called wisdom, and Holly dried her tears. But the event stuck in my craw, causing me to withdraw from the woman.

A year later, at a party, my former friend made a sarcastic remark about my feeble photography abilities. I immediately found something to do on the other side of the room. Later, she came into the kitchen, all smiles, to invite me to her church concert. My polite decline prompted her to demand an explanation for what she called my bad attitude over the previous year. When I offered the door-closing scene as an explanation, she denied it, saying there was no way she ever would have done anything like that to Holly.

Negative memories can be repressed to the point that a person truly has no recollection of them.

I was bewildered. Holly isn't a liar, but neither is the woman. What had happened? How could I offer forgiveness for something she insisted never happened? In my Colorado Springs quest to find out, I discovered Dr. Robert Coutts and his wife, Mary, who were working in the area of neuropsychology. As we talked about brain chemistry, I learned negative memories can be repressed to the point that a person truly has no recollection of them.

To illustrate the brain's power to dismiss painful memories, Dr. Coutts told me about one of his counseling sessions in which a mother called her adult son, who also was in the meeting, the world's worst in his particular profession. The son fretted about his mother's comment for several days and couldn't wait to discuss it at the next session. But when Dr. Coutts asked the mother about it the following week, she insisted she never would have said anything that hurtful to her son. I was fascinated by his account. The door-closing incident was so important to Holly and me that we remembered it, but the woman truly had forgotten it.

Did I bother to share this new information with her? No. But knowing about brain chemistry helped me forgive her. And it also taught me to settle future misunderstandings immediately instead of letting them fester within my spirit.

The Bible offers an example of the benefits of confronting someone directly. First Samuel 1:1–17 relates the story of Hannah and Eli. Hannah had no children, unlike her husband's other wife, Peninnah. One year, during the annual trek to the temple, Hannah, in anguish, prayed silently, asking for a child. The priest, Eli, misunderstood and wrongly accused her of being drunk. Think about that: She was doing the right thing, and she was misunderstood.

When Eli accused her of drunkenness, Hannah had several choices. She could lash out in anger; she could tearfully slip away, crying about being wrongly accused; or she could choose a third and correct response: communicate directly with her accuser. She chose the latter.

At Eli's accusation, Hannah replied, "Not so, my lord . . . I am a woman who is deeply troubled. I have not been drinking wine or beer; I was pouring out my soul to the Lord" (v. 15). Eli then said, "Go in peace, and may the God of Israel grant you what you have asked of him" (v. 17). Sometime later, Hannah became pregnant.

What a wonderful example her story is. Not only is immediate communication the key to avoiding petty misunderstandings that can grow into monsters, but it also may provide a much needed blessing.

And we all need that!

Prayer: Father God, you know I want emotional freedom. But forgiving the ones who have hurt me seems impossible. I confess I want them punished. I want them to hurt as much as they have hurt me. Sigh. But what good will that do? Yes, as always, I'm going to need your help as I travel this emotional road.

Thoughts to Ponder

1. What situations or people do you need to forgive for your own sake?
2. Are you comfortable with making an actual list and then saying, "I forgive" over each one?
3. If you aren't comfortable making that list yet, do you think you might be someday?

Personal Ponderings

Forgiving Ourselves

Day 17

And Asking Others to Forgive Us

For the sake of your name, O LORD, forgive my iniquity, though it is great. Psalm 25:11

Okay, we're willing to consider forgiving others for our own sake, but what about the times we can't forgive ourselves for some previous action? One mother berates herself for not going to her son's wedding. A young friend wishes she had never gotten an abortion. Another friend said she should have tried harder at her marriage. A coworker blames herself for her daughter's drug addiction. The list of regrets and heartbreak is endless.

We can quote 1 John 1:9—"If we confess our sins, he is faithful and just and will forgive us our sins and purify us from all unrighteousness"—to ourselves until we're purple, but nothing will change if we don't take that Scripture to heart. Yes, all too often we won't accept the forgiveness our heavenly Father offers, choosing to let the Enemy torment us with our past actions. I understand. In fact, I remember agonizing over a decision I'd made years ago. Without giving details, I mentioned my struggle to a coworker.

He listened, then picked up his mug. As he headed to the kitchenette to get coffee, he said, "Remember that you made your decision based on the information you had at the time."

He undoubtedly didn't give it another thought as he strolled toward the coffee urn, but I stood in my office doorway marveling at the relief that dropped around my shoulders like a comforting Kentucky quilt.

"When we confess our sins, God throws them into the deepest part of the sea and puts up a No Fishing sign."

Soon after his comment, my interest in church history introduced me to the sixteenth-century Heidelberg Catechism of the Reformed Churches. Question 56 immediately grabbed my attention: "Question: What do you believe concerning the forgiveness of sins? Answer: That for the sake of Christ's reconciling work, God will no more remember my sins or the sinfulness with which I have to struggle all of my life long; but that he graciously imparts to me the righteousness of Christ so that I may never come into condemnation."

Corrie ten Boom put this concept of forgiveness into a simpler form: "When we confess our sins, God throws them into the deepest part of the sea and puts up a No Fishing sign."

In addition to forgiving others and ourselves, a third tough issue exists: asking for forgiveness from others. Ouch, huh? I remember cringing each time I thought of an event from my college years. Finally, I decided I had to apologize. I confess my motivation wasn't pure. Even though I knew apologizing was the right thing to do, I was more interested in being at peace. So finally I took a deep breath, yelped a simple prayer of "Please help," and dialed the number. I held my breath as I listened to the phone ring, hoping no one would be home. But on

> *I took a deep breath, yelped a simple prayer of "Please help," and dialed the number.*

the fourth ring, I heard a cheery "Hello." I immediately babbled an apology, expecting to hear a solid slamming of the receiver. I'd already decided that would be fine; at least I would have done what I was supposed to do. But the recipient of my apology did not hang up, and we talked for more than an hour, clearing up an old misunderstanding and giving me peace.

But what if we need to ask forgiveness from someone who has died? Two solutions come to mind: writing and praying. Several years ago when I was part of a grief counseling team for a Detroit funeral home chain, I listened to numerous folks express regrets about what they wish they had said to the deceased or wish they could undo. Sometimes we gave them the assignment to visit the grave and talk to the ground. Sometimes we asked them to pretend the person was seated nearby. Usually, though, we asked them to write that person a heartfelt letter. If they were people of faith, we suggested they pray and ask the Lord to pass along the message.

I confess that when our head counselor first suggested these activities, I was skeptical. And I probably rolled my eyes because he challenged me to write my own letter to someone deceased. The name of a long-dead relative came to mind immediately, so I sighed and opened my notebook. I planned to write a quick paragraph or two, but three pages later I finished my apology. And I had a new understanding of the power of forgiveness.

> *Prayer: Father God, I wish the serious issues of life weren't so difficult. I confess I don't have any trouble dwelling on what other people have done to me. But I don't like looking at the areas where I've been wrong. Dealing with those is going to take a while, so I ask for your help.*

Thoughts to Ponder

1. What past actions do you regret?
2. Have you ever apologized for an action? If so, what happened?
3. Are you comfortable with writing an apology letter to a deceased person? Why or why not?

Personal Ponderings

Analyze and Adjust
Look for New Adventures

> Those who trust in the LORD are like Mount Zion, which cannot be shaken but endures forever. As the mountains surround Jerusalem, so the LORD surrounds his people both now and forevermore. Psalm 125:1–2

D o you ever compare yourself to others? Me too. And since I know that tendency all too well, I know the trick is to get those comparisons going in the right direction. Thus, over the years I've learned to focus not on folks who seemingly have everything but on those who need help. And by reaching out to others, my children and I learned to concentrate on what we had left instead of lamenting what we had lost.

That first Thanksgiving after being thrust into single parenting, I decided not to cook the big meal I had prepared in the past. And I didn't accept any of the invitations we received. I knew being with complete families would intensify my feelings of loss.

So I called the local Salvation Army and asked if we could help serve dinner. Amazingly, even that small service to homeless veterans, transient workers, or even other single-parent families helped us far more than it helped those on the receiving end. And afterward, the three of us went home with a special feeling of peace.

The day had its humorous moments too. I'd told Jay and Holly not to wear their nicest clothes since I didn't want us to look as though we condescendingly were doing our good deed for the year. They apparently followed my instructions too well.

After we had served everyone else, we sat down with our own filled plates. Just as we lifted our heads from prayer, a photographer from the local paper stepped through the doorway. He surveyed the room, spotted my youngsters, smiled, and came over.

"I'm from the paper, and we're doing a story on families having dinner at the Salvation Army," he said. "May I take your picture? This will be a great shot—you and your kids."

I panicked. "Oh, no! We're volunteers. We've been serving dinner to the others."

He smiled gently. "It's okay. Everybody needs a little help now and then."

"But we're volunteers," I insisted. "We came to help."

An older gentleman at the next table had been watching the scenario. "You can take *my* picture," he said. "I won't make as pretty a one as the youngins, but I'll smile fer you."

The photographer shrugged and snapped one shot of the man before moving to the other side of the room. I decided next year I'd let Jay and Holly wear their nicest sweaters.

> *He smiled gently. "It's okay. Everybody needs a little help now and then."*

But I also had to face an area deep within my being I hadn't known was there—pride that we were helping instead of being helped. Even all these years later, I analyze my reaction. Yes, I'm grateful for the service opportunity that propelled me out of my self-pity, but I'm also aware the photographer was right when he said, "Everybody needs a little help now and then." So don't let pride keep you from getting any help your family may need.

While I was finding new ways to serve others, I also had to learn how to assume the responsibilities that once had been my husband's. Most single moms hear at least occasionally, "Daddy didn't do it that way," whether they're making French toast or cleaning the garage.

When Melanie's children made these comments, she used to snap, "Well, Daddy's not here!" But she soon realized such a retort only deepened the gloom. Finally she forced herself to ask them to show her "how Daddy would do this." To her delight, Jimmy, her twelve-year-old son, remembered how to pour the gasoline into the lawn mower tank without splashing. Soon she was asking Jimmy how *he* would tackle a task.

While we're learning new tasks, we need to allow ourselves to have fun. We can become so worried about paying bills, making friends, settling into a new routine that we miss the joy of *this* moment. That was a tough area for me because I don't like change. The familiar was my security blanket, and I liked having it tightly wrapped around me.

> *But I also had to face an area deep within my being I hadn't known was there—pride that we were helping instead of being helped.*

But single parenting snatched away that security, shoving me into new territory. The only healthy choice I could make was to analyze the situation and then find ways to adjust. But once I forced myself to take little risks, even changing my basic wardrobe color from the pinks my husband bought for me to the deep purples I'd always loved, I discovered a heart for adventure.

That realization quickly translated into having fun with my young children, including garbage-bag tobogganing near their grandparents' home. I took to carrying a box of oversized plastic lawn bags in the car trunk for such impromptu romps.

Even a walk in the woods became an adventure. And looking back now, we recognize that our favorite memories from those early years of adjustment are in the unplanned events, such as trips to a cider mill or free art fairs, and not the trips I overplanned for weeks.

When I was married, Sunday afternoons revolved around football. If I wanted to invite folks for dinner, they had to like football. Now, these many years later, I confess that while I still miss my husband, I don't miss football one bit. As I reclaimed those fall and winter Sunday afternoons, I started looking for activities Jay, Holly, and I could do together. Free museums, plays, and orchestra concerts quickly filled the time once belonging to football.

The only healthy choice I could make was to analyze the situation and then find ways to adjust.

Those activities were some of our choices for a Sunday afternoon; they may not be yours. The point is, depending on your tastes, budget, and the ages of your children, do whatever appeals to you as a family. Maybe visiting with friends and relatives is more to your liking, or taking in a matinee or going to the zoo, or whatever.

If you're outdoor types, you've got hiking, biking, and romping in the park, as well as skating, sledding, and all the rest of those cold-weather sports when the temperature drops and the snow starts falling, as it did when we lived in Michigan. Whatever your climate, find new ways to enjoy being together.

Remember, analyze and adjust. We don't have to be victims of our circumstances.

Prayer: Father God, I don't like change. But here I am— dealing with one change after another. Please help me accept my new role even as I analyze our challenges and find new ways to celebrate being a family.

Thoughts to Ponder

1. What is the toughest part of your schedule now? What adjustments have you made?
2. What new activities do you and your children enjoy together?
3. What has surprised you the most as you try new adventures?

Personal Ponderings

_____

_____

_____

Day
19

Celebrate with Joy
Laughter Is Good Medicine

A cheerful heart is good medicine, but a crushed spirit dries up the bones. Proverbs 17:22

Altering the way we have always celebrated holidays is the best way to handle them, especially when we're facing the first ones as single moms.

Just after we moved to Colorado Springs, I had lunch with a new friend who was wading through an unwanted divorce. As she sipped her cola, she said, "I remember a guy in our office who said nobody invited him to their Christmas parties after his divorce. The holiday is still four months away, and already I'm wondering what I'm going to do."

I shrugged. "That's easy. You and your kiddos are having Christmas dinner with us."

She shook her head. "I can't do that. Remember? I have four children."

I shrugged again. "So? I'm roasting a turkey that day. And if y'all don't come for dinner, you'll have to come for leftovers."

Finally she accepted, but only after she insisted we go to her place for Thanksgiving. Suddenly her eyes sparkled at the thought of filling her home again.

Within a few weeks, her Thanksgiving guest list consisted of an interesting group of single parents and their children she teasingly called the Lost and Found Gang. We all hit it off so well I invited *all* of them to my home for a potluck Christmas dinner. Not only were both holidays filled with fun, but the Lost and Found Gang became the core of my social circle. And all because another single mother and I analyzed our situations and adjusted to new routines.

Adjustments don't have to come in big ways, though. Sometimes little actions provide healing. Years ago, preteen Jay and Holly argued over a small blue pillow when they watched TV. Then I saw fluffy teddy bears stacked in a store sale bin. Their tummies were just the size of that old blue pillow. I picked out a brown bear for Jay and a white one for Holly.

Maybe I'm stronger now because I allowed myself those evenings of hugging a fluffy bear.

Then as I turned away with my carefully chosen selections, another white bear, this one with a floppy arm, caught my eye. He was imperfect; no one would buy him. Suddenly, with a surge of kinship, I bought him and named him Ralph.

Many nights after my children had gone to bed, I sat on the sofa and hugged my broken bear. Anyone who's met me in the last few years can't imagine that scene, but maybe I'm stronger now because I allowed myself those evenings of hugging a fluffy bear.

Peggy would understand my action. Her week in the blue-suit office world had been rough. Now Saturday's chores loomed, it was raining, and both her kids had colds. She pulled on her sweatshirt, then noticed she had it on backward. She sighed and started to turn the logo to the front. Suddenly she grinned at her mirrored reflection and turned her sweat pants inside out before she tugged them on. Then she pulled her hair into a top knot and tied it with a pair of her daughter's lavender tights. Not only did she feel well dressed for the gloomy morning, but she had learned the power of the occasional tension-relieving "weird day."

Marlene knows we often have to force our way out of ruts. When things start to close in, she takes her children for a walk. Their assignment is to see how many different sounds they can identify. The idea is to do something different—and fun.

Maybe you are one of those who has to have things "just so." I used to be like that. But when the New York editorial job offer came and we moved into a small condo, the cost of living was so high on the East Coast I couldn't afford fancy decorating. So we slapped paint on the walls and moved in. Within a couple of days of unpacking our boxes, I had hung several Amish and Southern quilts on the living room walls to add brightness. Then on the awkward space next to the stairs, I hung the scatter rugs my Kentucky grandmother had braided years ago. Most of them were ones I had wiped my feet on at her backdoor years ago, never dreaming they'd someday move with me to that great end of the world—New York.

When everything was in place, I admired the splashes of color against the off-white paint. Magnificent! What I originally meant as a temporary solution quickly became my personal decorating signature. Those quilts later adorned my Colorado office and home as well. Often my visitors admire the fabric and say, "These quilts are so *you*." And truly they are.

Just as we need to adjust to new ways to celebrate holidays and find daily joys, we also need to give ourselves permission to laugh again. That's a tough area for the woman who unexpectedly finds herself a single mother, especially for those of us who had a somber childhood. In fact, it seemed to take *forever* before I could laugh again once life pitched me into single parenting. But laughter did return. I remember when it happened. A relative was giving an account of his encounter with a zany cousin. I've since forgotten the story he told, but I recall the corners of my mouth turning up as I listened. In that moment, I gave in to a rib-splitting laugh. And it felt good.

Laughter not only feels good, but it's good for our health. We know scientifically that the brain releases endorphins, the body's own medicine, when we laugh. And beyond relieving daily tension, laughter creates wonderful memories—for us as well as for our youngsters. One of my elderly friends says she never heard her grandmother laugh and seldom saw her smile except at other adults. How sad. Let's make sure our children won't carry such memories.

Just as we need to adjust to new ways to celebrate holidays and find daily joys, we also need to give ourselves permission to laugh again.

Laura's children were four and three when their dad took off. Laughing was the last thing she wanted to do, but she also knew she couldn't sit despondently in a darkened house and expect the children to be quiet and somber too. One evening, in desperation, she draped a blanket over a card table and suggested the children play tent.

Soon the four-year-old peeked from under the table and gestured for Laura to join them. She started to say, "No, you just play." But to her own surprise, she said, "Sure!"

For the next hour Laura enjoyed her children's laughter and even found herself strengthened by it. Truly, the cheeriness of their time together was good medicine for them all.

Prayer: Father God, creating fun for us is the last thing on my to-do list. But if it's important, I guess I need to think about it. I'm gonna need your help big time, though. Please help me see beauty and even fun in each new day. And help me show it to my children too.

Thoughts to Ponder

1. What are the toughest parts of the holidays for you now?
2. Have you been pleasantly surprised by one of your seemingly small adjustments?
3. What do you and your children enjoy doing together for fun?

Personal Ponderings

Take Care
of Your Health

A *Personal Lesson*

Dear friend, I pray that you may enjoy good health and that all may go well with you, even as your soul is getting along well. 3 John 1:2

This is one of those "Do as I say and not as I do" sections. I've always been ready to take care of other people, but taking care of myself? Well, that's a different matter. Thus, my weight crept up—and sometimes rushed in—and on the list of priorities, my own health was always at the bottom. That is, until I finally landed in a hospital emergency room.

At the time, I was associate editor for a Christian magazine in New York and putting in long hours. We desperately needed a secretary to handle the volume of daily mail. My boss had asked the powers that be to get us some help, but the response came down that I was handling being both secretary and editor just fine.

So September 28 had to happen, sooner or later.

That day, we had our usual intense schedule: Everything was going wrong, deadlines were missed, and two readers had called, wanting to talk to someone about decisions they were facing in their own lives. With my grief counseling background, I usually wound up taking those calls. Then just about 4:00 p.m., the overnight courier called, saying they'd lost the artwork for the next issue. I numbly heard only that they would continue to check the warehouse. Next, the accounting department needed me. I got halfway up the stairs when my heart threatened to pound out of my rapidly tightening chest. All the invisible balls I'd been juggling suddenly clattered at my feet. I couldn't breathe. I eased down on the step, convinced I was having a heart attack.

After several minutes of sitting there on the staircase and praying, my heart pounding eased enough that I went on to the accounting office.

"Are you all right?" was my friend's quick question.

I nodded. "I'm just tired. It's been a long day."

Quitting time finally arrived, and I called Holly to let her know I'd be late coming home. Then I drove myself—not a bright idea, by the way—directly to the local hospital. The examining doctor quickly set me up for an EKG (electrocardiogram). Believe me, something about having wires attached to my chest and hooked up to machines that beeped every few moments put life into proper perspective.

My blood pressure was so dangerously high the doctor suddenly was more concerned about my having a stroke than he was about my having a heart attack. He gave me bitter medicine to hold under my tongue, while I kept wondering how Jay and Holly would get along if something happened to me.

> *Believe me, something about having wires attached to my chest and hooked up to machines that beeped every few moments put life into proper perspective.*

After two hours of running tests, deciding I wasn't having a heart attack after all, and bringing my blood pressure down to the high end of normal range, the doctor gave me the name of a heart specialist for follow-up examinations.

Then he said, "Tell me about your life."

I gave him a wry smile. "Not much to tell. I'm a single mom, raising two teens alone and putting in twelve- to sixteen-hour days on the job."

He nodded. "Want me to admit you here for a few days so you can catch your breath?"

I shook my head. "No. I'll sleep better in my own bed. But I promise to stay home from work tomorrow and see the specialist as soon as I can get an appointment."

> *Heaven is not here. Not any place on this earth. No matter where we live, we're going to have challenges.*

He let me go then. And the moment I walked out the hospital door, I mentally left New York, knowing it was just a matter of time until I tried to take back control of my life. But even the move to a new state and a new job didn't lessen all my stress and solve all my problems.

Know what I've learned? Heaven is not here. Not any place on this earth. No matter where we live, we're going to have challenges. And those challenges will force us to make important choices concerning our children—and ourselves. So wherever you are and whatever your situation, ask the Lord to show you ways to lighten your load so you can take care of yourself just as you are taking care of your children. You deserve to do that. And your children deserve a healthy mom.

Prayer: Father God, in my sad moments I'm prone to think no one ever took care of me, so I don't know how to take care of myself. But I'm willing to learn, starting in little ways right now. I know my children need me, and I realize how much I need you to help me in this area. In fact, in all areas.

Thoughts to Ponder

1. How's your health? Do you have areas you'd like to improve?
2. What's your biggest challenge for taking care of your health?
3. What do you think about the statement that no matter where we live, we're going to have challenges?

Personal Ponderings

Day 21 Keep Your Children Talking

And Keep Listening

Rejoice with those who rejoice; mourn with those who mourn.
Romans 12:15

Rain had fallen for several days on President Thomas Jefferson and his party as they traveled cross-country on horseback. In their journeying, they reached the river they were to cross and found the rain-swollen waters had swept away the only bridge. The president and his entourage meandered up and down the riverbank until they discovered a place where their horses could cross safely. Nearby, a man sat hunched under a tree. As the group approached, he stood and looked at each man.

Then he spoke to President Jefferson. "Please, sir, will you carry me across with you?"

President Jefferson nodded and helped the man swing up behind him. When they arrived safely on the far bank, the man jumped down and offered his thanks.

One of Jefferson's escorts turned to the now-dismounted rider and challenged him.

"How is it you dared to ask to ride behind the president of the United States?"

The man blanched, looked into the kind face of his benefactor, then faced his questioner.

"I didn't know I was speaking to the president," he said. "It's just that I saw *no* in your faces and *yes* in his."

Former Colorado pastor John Stevens told that story years ago, but the important theme has stayed with me. After all, that's what communication with our children should be—making sure they see *yes* in our faces and know we are approachable. Despite our intense schedules and personal worries, we must create an atmosphere in our homes that invites our sons and daughters to talk to us about anything and safely share their concerns.

> *Kids aren't going to listen to our words if our facial expressions announce disapproval.*

We know what says no to teens: putdowns, sarcasm, orders, "you should" statements, and impatience that cuts them off in midsentence.

So what makes for approachability?

For starters, offer sincere compliments when appropriate. I remember neighbors who thought complimenting their children would spoil them. So they never said, "Good job, honey," after a long day of chores. Sadly, that resulted in children who grew into teens looking for validation from others—sometimes with disastrous consequences.

True, we need to have rules, set boundaries, and say no at times. But even then we don't have to be negative or overly critical. Kids aren't going to listen to our words if our facial expressions announce disapproval of everything they do. Most kids really do want to do it right.

The late West Coast counselor Jean Lush said when she worked with her father she felt as though she could do anything. He told funny stories, offered lavish praise, and made his four children feel as though they were the greatest kids in the world. Her mother, however, was frustrated by their fumbling efforts and often compared them to their aunt Ida, the family misfit.

Guess which parent's requests were answered with enthusiasm?

> *The human mind often has to mull over a thought, talk about it, put it aside, and then talk about it again.*

Mrs. Lush also liked to remind single moms that many of the world's great leaders and scientists were raised only by their mothers. A welcome thought!

By the way, remember that just because children don't talk doesn't mean they aren't hurting. In fact, those may be the very ones who are carrying the greatest pain. So find ways to spend one-on-one time together. You might even come up with the rule that they take turns helping you prepare dinner. Working together forces us to talk.

But don't expect to solve all of life's problems with one intense conversation. The human mind often has to mull over a thought, talk about it, put it aside, and then talk about it again.

Chris said that, after her divorce, her sons were so relieved their father's abuse would stop that at first they didn't seem to need or want to talk. But gradually over the next year, they needed to sort through issues again. Chris alternated taking a short walk with each son after dinner to provide that opportunity and answer their long-held questions.

> *I casually added "What would you do if" questions into our conversations.*

Walks worked for us too—especially as I casually added "What would you do if" questions into our conversations.

When my children were four and five, the questions were about basic protection: "What would you do if a car pulled up and the driver asked you to approach?"

As they got older, the questions progressed to whatever they might be dealing with in school: "What would you do if your best friend forgot to study for the math test and asked you to keep your paper uncovered?"

Once I had asked the question, I waited instead of offering immediate motherly wisdom. If they didn't have a solution, then I could offer my own suggestions in what I hoped was a casual, nonjudgmental way. My goal was to get my kiddos to plan good responses before facing the actual situation.

Occasionally, I'd even give them an opportunity to comment on my parenting. For example, one Sunday I impulsively asked, "What do you wish I'd do differently?"

Holly shrugged, but Jay immediately had a suggestion. "I wish you liked science more."

I nodded. "I wish I did too. But we both know that isn't going to happen anytime soon. Meanwhile, how about if we go to the local science museum?"

That proved exactly the right thing to do. Every few weeks, we'd meander past the latest displays, while Jay explained what we were seeing. Occasionally, I even understood enough to ask a question. I never did get excited about molecules and atoms, but those trips were important to my son and, thus, important to me.

Once Jay and Holly hit their teens, my questions got even more specific:

"What would you do if you were at a party and someone offered you drugs?"

"What would you do if your date said his or her parents were away for the weekend and suggested you go over there?"

Neither of my children had to run from the stranger in the car, but they were both asked to cheat, offered drugs, and propositioned.

I'm grateful they handled those situations well. I know it was God's mercy and answered prayers that got them safely through, but this tired single mother still likes to think some of my "What would you do if" questions paid off.

Prayer: Father God, it's difficult to be patient when faced with my child's bad attitude and eye-rolling. Help me take a deep breath and put yes on my face as we talk. And help me remember that yes always is on your face when I talk to you.

Thoughts to Ponder

1. What's your reaction to the story about the man who saw *yes* in President Jefferson's face but *no* in the faces of his companions?
2. What do you and your children talk about most?
3. Are you comfortable asking your children what they would like you to do differently as the parent? Why or why not?

Personal Ponderings

Choose Your Battles

Day 22

Don't Die on Every Hill

> But the fruit of the Spirit is love, joy, peace, forbearance, kindness, goodness, faithfulness, gentleness and self-control. Against such things there is no law. Galatians 5:22–23

The above Scripture presents quite a challenge, doesn't it? But how are we supposed to display all those spiritual qualities when we're raising children alone—especially if they are teenagers? We take a deep breath, invite our heavenly Father into every day, and pick our battles carefully. In other words, we don't overreact to every decision our kiddos make.

In his mid-teens, Jay became intrigued by his Scottish heritage and even wore the kilt made from his family tartan to formal school functions. During this time, he also discovered a wood carving of a rugged clansman. Hanging over one shoulder was a single, long braid.

As soon as Jay showed me the carving, I knew what he planned to do.

"I don't care if you grow your hair to your knees," I said. "Just keep it clean."

He was active in the youth group and still attending the worship service, so I didn't think much more about it. But as the months wore on, I realized folks at our church and at my conservative workplace were judging *me* for Jay's long hair.

Single moms have enough spiritual battles without accepting false ones, so I shrugged off the comments by saying, "If my hair were the color of Scottish gold, I'd grow it out too."

Often the church loses youngsters by insisting they be clones instead of helping them discover who they are in Jesus.

Besides, I knew his male relatives had balded early, so I wanted him to enjoy having hair while he could.

The most frustrating comments came from some Bible colleges that called to invite Jay to the campus for the day. As soon as he would tell the callers about his hair, their first question to him wasn't "Do you want to know more about the Lord?" but "Are you willing to cut your hair?"

Isn't it a pity we live in a world so concerned about outward appearance? Often the church loses youngsters by insisting they be clones instead of helping them discover who they are in Jesus.

Anyway, Jay finally decided to attend a state university renowned for its chemistry department. With that decision made, he promptly cut his hair!

When I questioned him, he merely shrugged. "It's time," he said.

So, Mom, take heart and don't battle over unimportant issues. Instead, battle issues like drugs and alcohol, not hair length, neatness of rooms, or music choices (unless they are obscene). And say yes as often as possible; it gives more credibility to the times when you must say no.

Dr. James Dobson has written about the waitress who told him of the ongoing battle she and her twelve-year-old daughter were having about the girl wanting to shave her legs. They'd had a miserable year because of that raging discussion, and the mother didn't know what to do.

What would the famous psychologist suggest?

Dr. Dobson looked at her and said, "Buy her a razor!"

Too often we're so busy trying to make our teens do what we think is important that we don't listen to what is important to them. Yes, I know we're trying to impart our vast, hard-earned wisdom. If only they'd listen, we think, they wouldn't suffer sad consequences. But if we expect them to listen to us, we must listen to them.

> *Too often we're so busy trying to make our teens do what we think is important that we don't listen to what is important to them.*

One thing that will help ease that tension is to remember what worked for us when we were younger. Most of us learned through our mistakes. Why? Because even when our parents tried to warn us, most of us thought we were merely being lectured. And we ended up learning tough lessons the hard way.

One mother realized during yet another of her well-meaning but stern lectures how her demands must have sounded to her sixteen-year-old daughter. She took a deep breath and quietly said, "Where you're going, I have been." That simple statement opened the emotional door to less yelling and more honest communication.

As both a mother and a high school teacher, one of my constant themes was, "These are *not* the best years of your life! They *will* get better—if you let them." Of course, wrong choices about drugs, alcohol, friends, and sexual activity will alter a bright future.

My students always seemed relieved when I'd assure them a brighter future awaited, but invariably someone would ask, "So why do our folks always say these are such great years?"

The obvious answer is that teens have choices. The older we get, the more limited our choices become. But in an emotional moment, adults often have trouble verbalizing that fact. So let's listen before we lecture, trust that good days *are* ahead, and remember to keep *yes* on our faces.

Prayer: Father God, I want to protect my children from . . . everything. But our arguments and my lectures aren't solving anything. So help me take a deep breath, listen to you, and then listen to my children.

Thoughts to Ponder

1. Have you ever been judged because of your children's decisions or actions?
2. If your children are old enough to argue, what do you and they disagree about?
3. What helps you the most when you face challenges from either your children or others?

Personal Ponderings

Their Questions Matter

Honest Answers Wanted

May these words of my mouth and this meditation of my heart be pleasing in your sight, Lord, my Rock and my Redeemer. Psalm 19:14

Have your children ever asked about events either within the family or our nation you'd rather not revisit? Mine have. Yes, I've had to reveal a few family secrets, but one national event was especially difficult to discuss—the Vietnam War. Jay had overheard me tell a New York friend that I'd worked as a civilian secretary for a Reserve Officers' Training Corps (ROTC) unit at the end of the war, so he asked about the antiwar riots that had shut down our college. As I remembered those intense days, I included details of my own conservative attitude until Clive, the handsome senior I sighed over in high school study hall, came home in a body bag.

But I still couldn't describe the craziness of those years or what it was like for our soldiers not to know who the enemy was. Finally, I took teenage Jay to see the movie *Good Morning, Vietnam*. The plot explained that era with far greater impact than I could have.

Later, as we lingered over soft drinks, I talked about three of my classmates who died in the war. I described Clive's farm ambitions, Bob's football skill, and Scott's mathematical awards. But Jay still had questions. I could have introduced him to the war section of our local library, but since we were just a few hours north of Washington, DC, I drove the three of us there the next school break to see the Vietnam Veterans Memorial Wall.

How do I describe the sight of the Wall with more than fifty-six thousand names of the war dead carved into panels of black granite?

On the main sidewalk, two vets looked up specific names in the thick directory they carried.

Nearby, a scoutmaster had a rowdy youngster by the lapels, saying, "Some of them were my friends. Someday you'll understand what you've seen here."

A father lifted his toddler to touch a name, whispering, "No, put your hand just a little higher. There! That's your grandpa."

I wept as I thought of that toddler's grandfather, who probably had been in his early twenties when he died, leaving behind a son who was little older than the child he now held up.

As we left the Wall, Jay looked at me. "Thanks, Mom," was all he said.

I realize not everyone lives within a few hours of our nation's capital, but important history can be found in every community and in every family. Think of ways to invite your children into those important local and personal events.

Yes, you may want to postpone telling family secrets for a while, depending on your child's age, but don't shrug at what your children want to talk about— whether it's a sad event in our nation's history or having to eat lunch alone at school when a best friend is sick. I do

> *Every time we dismiss what our children think is important, we close the door of communication on their future problems.*

agree that with all we're juggling daily, it's tempting to dismiss what we see as unimportant. But every time we dismiss what our children think is important, we close the door of communication on their future problems.

Jenna's eleven-year-old daughter chattered constantly, telling her every detail of the school day, including what her friends wore, what they ate for lunch, and what they talked about. After one especially long work day, Jenna didn't know if she could listen to one more account of who spilled pudding on the cafeteria floor. But she decided if she wanted her daughter to talk to her when she was dating as a teen, she'd better listen to boring details *now*.

> *She decided if she wanted her daughter to talk to her when she was dating as a teen, she'd better listen to boring details* now.

So this tired mother took a deep breath and said, "Let's take turns. For fifteen minutes, you tell me what happened at school. Then I'll tell you in fifteen minutes what happened at work today."

Not only did the exchange give Jenna a chance to vent her own disappointment over not being invited to a briefing meeting, but it gave her daughter a glimpse into the hassles her mother was dealing with every day too.

Perhaps your children don't talk about school, but you wish they would. So ask questions about their teachers, their classmates, their favorite subjects. Yes, that takes effort, but school takes up most of their day, and their peers take up most of their thoughts. I'm convinced listening to our youngsters and talking about their concerns is another way we can say, "I love you."

Prayer: Father God, you know the things I hope my children never ask about— within both my past and our nation's history. But if I have to deal with those events someday, I guess I should start talking to you about them now. And when I talk to my children about them, I trust you to help me.

Thoughts to Ponder

1. What national events would you rather not discuss with your children?
2. What personal experiences do you hope your children never ask about?
3. Are you comfortable talking to the Lord about both of those issues now in preparation for a potential future discussion with your children?

Personal Ponderings

Day 24

Gracious Words

Breathe Deeply, Pray Often

Gracious words are a honeycomb, sweet to the soul and healing to the bones. Proverbs 16:24

What do you tell your children about their father? Widows often speak of only his good qualities. One of my friends did that too well; her son refused to play football, thinking he'd never be as good as his dad.

Divorced moms have to fight the other extreme of talking about only his undesirable qualities. But Diane made a better choice when she introduced her fifteen-year-old son when he stopped by our workplace. As we chatted, he said, "Some people think I look like my mother. But I don't think so, do you?"

Before I could answer, Diane smiled and said, "No, you look like your dad."

Then she turned to me. "His dad is a fox! That's why I married him."

As her son shyly smiled, I thought about Diane's bitter divorce and marveled she didn't transfer that pain to her son with a sarcastic comment about his looking like his father. Instead, her words were a gift to her son, just as today's Scripture says.

Her words were a gift to her son.

Another gift to give a child is the refusal to transfer blame. Renee, even as an adult, is convinced she caused her parents' marriage to fail. She still remembers the evening she timidly approached her crying mother with, "Why did Daddy leave?"

Her mother's answer? "Everything was fine until you came along!"

So let's determine to bite back stinging comments and concentrate on getting through each day. This restraint is especially important if the child spends weekends with the dad.

When Claire packed overnight bags for her children's first weekend away, she put masking tape over her mouth to keep from saying the bitter things she was thinking.

"My kids thought it was a game and put tape on their mouths too," she says. "We all looked pretty silly, but it helped me get through the packing and gave them a fun memory."

Ah, memories. One of my favorites is of my Kentucky grandparents kneeling in their living room each evening and praying aloud at the same time. I'd try to pray too, but I was so intrigued by the thought of God sorting their voices I'd never get through my own petitions.

I wonder what memories of prayer Jay and Holly will carry into their adulthood. I'd like it to be of the prayers and Scripture after dinner, but it probably will be the times when I began with, "Lord, you know I hate days like this."

Connie says her mother's prayers followed her in California during the 1960s hippie era.

Connie says her mother's prayers followed her in California during the 1960s hippie era.

"No matter where I was or what I was doing, I knew she was praying for me," Connie says. "The memory of her kneeling by her bed with an open Bible just wouldn't leave me. Now that I'm raising my daughter alone, I want her to talk to God as easily as she talks to me. That means she has to see me doing it too."

But what if praying with another person is new to you?

You take a deep breath for courage and tell your children you'd like them to join you in talking to God together. Sometimes, though, you don't have time to discuss it first. Vina had felt awkward about praying aloud, but when her teen daughter threatened to move out, she grabbed her in a bear hug and prayed aloud, "Lord, help me show this special little gal I really do love her. Amen."

Her daughter looked up at Vina. "How come you've never prayed with me before?"

"I want her to talk to God as easily as she talks to me."

When Vina stammered, "I guess I was afraid," the daughter hugged her again. Finally they were communicating on a level the teen could understand.

And isn't that the goal we all share?

Prayer: Father God, help me choose the right words as I talk to my children about their dad. Help me talk to you about everything. Help me show my children how to talk to you. May they hear my love—and yours.

Thoughts to Ponder

1. What thoughts do you have about the father of your children?
2. What's your greatest challenge as you talk to your children about their dad?
3. Are you comfortable praying with your children? Why or why not?

Personal Ponderings

_____

_____

_____

Guiding Teens through Sexual Waters

Day 25

No Room for Denial

No temptation has overtaken you except what is common to mankind. And God is faithful; he will not let you be tempted beyond what you can bear. But when you are tempted, he will also provide a way out so that you can ensure it. 1 Corinthians 10:13

I f your children are little, you probably aren't anticipating their dating yet. But that time arrives sooner than we want, so how involved do you plan to be in their dating decisions?

I remember a friend's son who fathered two children with two girls when he was only fifteen! Argh! Jay and Holly always dreaded my hearing about someone getting in trouble; they knew they would have to hear the I'm-tough-for-a-reason lecture. This time was no different, but only Holly was home at the moment.

As I finished the report, I said when she started dating, I'd have to meet each date before the event, and if I didn't like him, she wasn't going out with him.

She rolled her eyes and muttered that I'd forgotten what it was like to be a teen. I pounced on her words. "No, Holly. I'm tough because I *do* remember."

These days of sexual permissiveness and low moral standards are frightening for parents of teens. But we can't pretend our children won't be tempted when the hormones hit. And we can't ignore the fact that so many young lives are disrupted and even ruined in a few moments.

In my first year of teaching, two bright fifteen-year-old students in my English class created a baby. To this day, both wonder about the child they placed for adoption. Other students went away for long weekends to get abortions—and turned to drugs or alcohol to deaden the resulting emotional pain. Other times, girls cried as they told me they were pregnant.

One sophomore said, "But I don't think I'm *really* pregnant. We did it for just a couple of seconds." Another student said she'd "done it" only once. But once was all it took.

The girls and I would talk, and I'd offer to go with them to tell their parents, but no one ever took me up on that. I'd watch them leave with slumped shoulders, and then *I'd* cry.

Though I'm no longer the concerned teacher, I'm a mom who had to be careful my memories of those students and my fears didn't cloud my own children's dating.

Of course, it's tough trying to keep our teens on the straight and narrow. And, I confess, the best year for me as a single mom of teens was when Jay was fifteen and Holly fourteen—because he couldn't drive and she couldn't date! But this challenging time doesn't have to overwhelm us—as long as we keep our own standards high and keep talking to our teens about theirs. And it doesn't matter what their friends' parents say. I remember one mother who decided her own sexual activity limited any advice she could offer about abstinence. So when her teens started dating, she bought a large, clear-glass cookie jar and filled it with individually wrapped condoms. Her only comment about the jar was that she'd replenish the supply as needed. What a sad message.

> *The best year for me as a single mom of teens was when Jay was fifteen and Holly fourteen— because he couldn't drive and she couldn't date!*

We are the parents, and it's up to us to provide the guidance our teens need— and want. And we can't leave this area to the school professionals, either. After all, the only "safe sex" is no sex. The rates of sexually transmitted infections are alarming. And these modern infections are not the ones that were cured in past generations with a shot or two of penicillin. Today HIV/AIDS, herpes, genital warts—associated with HPV, which causes cervical cancer—are just a few of the infections awaiting new residences.

For too many single parents, their own sex education consisted of a horrified mother clutching at her blouse and reeling in mortification at innocent questions. Too often, the one caution offered us was a mysterious, "Be careful. Boys are after only one thing."

That universal warning really worried me as a young teen because I didn't know what that one thing was. I knew I didn't have any *money*.

I found out in due time, of course, so years later as a single mom, I tried to stress to my teens that sexual feelings are normal and, in fact, God-given, but our actions *can* be controlled.

> *These modern infections are not the ones that were cured in past generations with a shot or two of penicillin.*

When adults say, "Be careful your feelings don't run away with you," they're conveying the idea that sexual feelings are so strong they can overrule judgment. That's a wrong message. Sexual feelings don't have to be acted on any more than feelings of anger. Yes, we may not be able to control our feelings, but we *can* control our actions.

And so can our teens.

Prayer: Father God, how do I talk to my kids about sex when I have my own issues? Please help me listen to you and not to my fears. Help me protect and guide the children you have entrusted to me.

Thoughts to Ponder

1. Are you comfortable talking with your children about sex? Why or why not?
2. What are the greatest sexual challenges your children face—or will face later?
3. What are the greatest sexual challenges you face?

Personal Ponderings

Day 26

No Later Regrets
A Bright Future

But I will sing of your strength, in the morning I will sing of your love; for you are my fortress, my refuge in times of trouble. Psalm 59:16

I had been invited to speak on finding God's will at a college spiritual retreat. I went prepared with Scriptures and principles such as "God's direction for today never contradicts his Word" and "His call will be persistent." But the weekend proved to be an eye-opener for me; I hadn't expected to hear so many confessions—and regrets—from Christian young people.

On the second night, one of the girls sat on my bunk and sobbed her story of sexual activity, saying, "I want to go back to the way I was."

Another young woman told me her boyfriend had broken up with her after their intimacy. His reason? He was disappointed *she* hadn't been stronger.

My friend Rose is another speaker. Once she spoke at a California church gathering, emphasizing that good choices now prevent future regrets. Just then, in one of life's coincidences, the pastor entered the room and stood quietly in the back. Rose stared at him and, in bewilderment, called him by name.

He looked just as stunned at seeing her. "Rosie?" he said.

She turned back to the audience.

Are you smiling at a twelve-year-old's innocence? I did too.

"Back in Michigan, more than thirty years ago, I dated your pastor. How would we have felt seeing each other now if we had been intimate then?"

So how do we, as single mothers, help our teens set goals that will help them not have future regrets? By planning ahead.

A few months after Holly's twelfth birthday, she asked when she could start dating. I wanted to yell, "Never!" Instead, I calmly asked, "When do you think would be a good time?"

She thought for a moment, then said, "I think sixteen is a good age."

I wasted no time. "That's a good idea, Holly. Why don't we write that down, along with a few other thoughts?"

So we drew up what later would be known as "the Contract." We sat at the dining room table and discussed several situations. Then Holly carefully printed the following rules and expectations:

1. At 14, the start of freshman year, a boy can come over to do homework.
2. At 15, a parent drives for group dates.
3. No real dates until 16. Curfew will be 11:00 p.m. or time agreed to by Mom and Holly.
4. No kissing until 16 for party of Holly's choice.
5. No going steady until college.

6. No getting engaged until Holly's college senior year.

7. No marriage until Holly's college degree is complete.

8. Rules may be added to this list.

Are you smiling at a twelve-year-old's innocence? I did too.

After Holly finished listing the rules we had agreed upon, she wrote the date at the top of the paper, and we both signed it. I folded it and put it in a safe place. I'd just bought myself several years of peace. Or so I thought.

Everything was going along just fine until middle school. To hear my daughter tell it, every girl in Fox Lane School was going steady by the time she was in eighth grade. When she'd insist that she too be allowed to date even though she was only fourteen, I'd calmly ask, "What does the Contract say, Holly?"

Often she stomped out of the room, muttering, "I'm never signing anything ever again."

Somehow we got through middle school, but I dreaded the approach of her freshman year and fifteenth birthday when she could group date. Sure enough, it wasn't long after her birthday that she and another fifteen-year-old, whom I'll call Adam, were the sweethearts of first-hour lunch.

> *Often she stomped out of the room, muttering, "I'm never signing anything ever again."*

I insisted upon meeting him before they went bowling with friends. He had the good sense to be nervous but gave me details about where they were going, which parent would drive, and when they'd return. I took a deep breath, knowing the next step was just around the corner.

In the following months, I could see from Holly's tension she was being pressured. Adam had known about Holly's determination she wouldn't kiss until her sixteenth birthday since she wanted her party.

But Adam thought he could change her mind. And he was being hostile to me, saying I had tricked Holly into signing something at twelve that had no relevance to real life.

One day, I came home with my briefcase packed with articles to be edited by the next morning. But Holly was aggravated, so I ignored the work. For the next hour and a half we talked about present decisions affecting future relationships.

In the following months, I could see from Holly's tension she was being pressured.

Holly informed me the normal procedure in her school was for the guy to ask the girl out for their first date, and then they'd kiss. She insisted she had waited all those months and was tired of having a "dumb contract" forcing her to wait longer.

"Fine, Holly," I finally said. "If you want to kiss him, go ahead. But remember, the deal was you'd get a Sweet Sixteen party only if it *is* a Sweet Sixteen party. Life's full of decisions. You can't have everything. Make your choice."

Believe it or not, she chose the party and asked him not to pressure her. I'd like to report he was impressed with her determination and respected her decision. But alas, he broke up with her and started dating her best friend.

By the way, where did she choose to have her party after all that tension, those long arguments, and that unnecessary emotion? At our home. Is it any wonder my hair began to turn gray early?

I realize this story sounds old-fashioned, but we parents have a responsibility to help our teens make good choices—not only for today but for the future. Be encouraged, however, that not every teen out there is sexually active. In fact, recently the beautiful daughter of a friend showed me her Promise Ring that reminds her of her vow not to have sex before marriage, do drugs, or drink.

The teens of this decade are not the only ones who have ever faced sexual pressure. And whether they voice it, they need—and want—our understanding and protection in their scary new world. Remember, we are the parents. It's up to us to provide guidance.

> *Prayer: Father God, peer pressure is intense these days. Yes, I've faced it, and sometimes I didn't make the right decisions. So please help me as I help my children. May all of us get safely through these years.*

Thoughts to Ponder

1. What were your greatest challenges as a teen?
2. Do today's teens face different challenges? Why or why not?
3. From what future regrets do you want to protect your children?

Personal Ponderings

Day
27

Meet Their Dates

A *Casual Chat*

Like apples of gold in settings of silver is a ruling rightly
given. Proverbs 25:11

Are your children old enough to date? If so, do you talk with
their dates? I did.

At the start of Holly's junior year, one of the guys on the
wrestling team asked her to go bowling. I had hoped to postpone
the Talk a few more months, but there he was—a handsome young
man with a neck like a tree trunk, asking to take my daughter out.

The Talk consisted of Holly's would-be date answering seemingly casual questions about his interests, previous residences, and
family background.

This young man was nervous as he answered my chatty questions. He kept glancing toward the stairway, wondering when Holly
would be ready.

I smiled. "It's okay. She'll be downstairs when this is over."

He sighed.

I gestured toward the window where we could see his blue car
parked in front of the house. "That's a nice car," I said. "Obviously,
you take good care of it. But what would you do if a stranger came
to your door one evening and asked if he could borrow it, even
adding he'd take good care of it."

The lad smiled in sudden understanding. "I'd tell him I'd have
to know him better."

I nodded. "Exactly. And you've shown up here, asking to take
my daughter out for the evening. Her value is far more precious
to me than your car is to you."

117

He nodded quickly.

"But even though we've met, I haven't known anything about you before we began this talk," I said. "Right now you think this is ridiculous, but I guarantee in a few years when a stranger comes to your door to take your future daughter out for the evening, you'll think of me and say, 'That old lady was right!'"

> *"It's like my mom says, 'You don't have to like it; you just have to do it.'"*

As he mulled over that thought, I continued. "Another thing: You two are going out just as friends, but I've lived long enough to know how quickly situations can change. So remember this: Treat Holly the way you hope some other guy is treating your future wife."

His eyes widened. I knew I'd hit my target.

Word got around the wrestling team. Soon, when another guy mentioned he was going to ask Holly out, the others warned him about the Talk. One wrestler told Holly he hoped I hadn't changed my mind, adding, "I had to go through it; I want the other guys to face your mom too."

Of course, they'd tell each other what I asked, so I always had to vary my questions.

Only one young man refused to meet me, so Holly told him not to call her again. "It's like my mom says, 'You don't have to like it; you just have to do it.'"

She later confessed she was glad I had the rule because the guy made her nervous. Of course, I appreciated her comment, but it also underscored the fact that she was depending on my in-charge parenting as her protection.

In case you're wondering, I met Jay's dates too, but usually over lunch at our home and without the tension. And I didn't terrorize the girls in the same way I had the wrestlers. Instead, I privately talked to my son about his responsibility in a dating setting.

Amazingly, though, those talks with the guys who wanted to date Holly were almost easy compared with the discussions Jay and I had. I remember when mothers had to teach their daughters to say no. Well, today's mothers have to encourage their *sons* to say no.

I confess at times part of me longed for the day when Jay and Holly would be adults and I wouldn't have to be so watchful. But my older friends laughed, telling me my job wouldn't be over even then. "You just wait until your children give you grandchildren," they'd say. Argh!

But over the years, I learned my prayers carry more power than my talking. So, believe me, I prayed *a lot* then—and continue to do so now.

Was my involvement in my teens' dating old-fashioned? Unrealistic? Perhaps. But I remember the high school students during my teaching days who didn't have curfews or involved parents. Those students were more apt to face addictions, sexually transmitted diseases, unplanned pregnancies, and regrettable abortions. My involvement with Jay's and Holly's dating choices came with no guarantees, but at least they knew I was being vigilant. Oh, I wanted to pretend they were above such temptations, but I knew better. We single moms may not get through this stage as well as we'd like, but by talking to our children—and the Lord—and being watchful, we increase the chance of fewer regrets.

> *I learned my prayers carry more power than my talking. So, believe me, I prayed a lot then—and continue to do so now.*

How do Jay and Holly feel about my rules now that they are adults? Amazingly, they are grateful for my mother-bear vigilance. Sure, they kid me about some of the questions I asked their dates, and Holly rolls her eyes as she tells her friends about my quiet stroll through the bowling alley when she was on her first group date. But they carry no regrets.

And isn't having no regrets our goal for our children and ourselves?

Prayer: Father God, I have mixed feelings about the Talk. Yes, I understand Sandra's concern because of her former students. But I'm not sure this would work for my family. So please give me your guidance as I continue to welcome my role as my children's protector.

Thoughts to Ponder

1. What's your reaction to the Talk?
2. Are you comfortable having a similar chat with your children's present or future dates?
3. How would your children react to their dates having to face the Talk?

Personal Ponderings

Battling the Bills
Winning That War

> Better a little with the fear of the LORD than great wealth with turmoil. Better a small serving of vegetables with love than a fattened calf with hatred. Proverbs 15:16–17

I have in my files a letter from another single mother, which arrived at the Focus on the Family office shortly after one of my appearances on the daily radio broadcast.

The letter begins, "Dear Dr. Dobson, I really resent Sandra Aldrich."

Then the sender went on to describe the financial chaos into which divorce had dropped her while I had been "left all that money."

What?! I'd been left money? Wow, I didn't know that. Suddenly, I was excited.

Obviously, I'm being a smart aleck. I know only too well I wasn't left a windfall.

But why had the writer of that letter resented me? Because she *assumed* she knew the truth. And in her own pain, she thought the rest of the world was better off than she was. No, it wasn't money left to me keeping my children and me off the streets when I was thrust into single parenting. It was my own hard-earned education.

Paychecks were saved for college fees. My first paying job was when I was thirteen; a retirement home needed kitchen help and was willing to overlook my age. Throughout high school and college, I worked as a janitor, waitress, summer sports director, secretary, babysitter, café dishwasher, and salad girl—to name just a few jobs. Stray coins on the sidewalk were found treasure.

So if you want to resent me, pick real reasons. Resent me for my education, though I worked my way through college when my friends were dropping out to buy nice cars and hike through Europe. Resent me for not having to go to court to ask permission to move out of state. Resent me for not having to share my children at holidays with an ex-husband and his new family. But please don't resent me because of an imaginary insurance check.

We all need the encouragement and strength veteran single mothers can offer.

Obviously, I hope you won't resent me at all. After all, our challenges as single mothers are intense no matter how we arrived at this status. And we all need the encouragement and strength veteran single mothers can offer.

Some folks might be upset over my including a financial discussion in this devotional, saying if my faith were sound I wouldn't worry about paying bills. My faith is intact, thank you, and I truly do believe God provides for his children. However, I'm also a believer in the old saying, "God gives every bird its food, but he doesn't throw it into the nest!"

Besides, I'm always amazed that the people who admonish single mothers not to worry about money usually are the very ones who don't have to worry themselves!

Other folks like to remind me that money is evil. Wrong. First Timothy 6:10 (KJV) says, "The *love* of money"—not money itself—"is the root of all evil."

Jesus paid for our sins on the cross, but it's up to us to pay our bills. And because the Lord understands we have bills to pay, he wants us to talk over our finances with him, just as we talk to him about everything else.

One discussion I trust you will have with him is about tithing, which is giving one-tenth of our income to support the Lord's work. Even though the tithe is based on Old Testament practice rather than New Testament rule, I believe this is our responsibility and privilege.

If you're convinced you can't give a monetary tithe right now, consider tithing your time or talent by teaching a Sunday school class or painting a mural for the nursery. The important thing is for us to give back to the Lord a portion of what he has given us.

A caution here, though: However we decide to pay our tithe, we should do so out of a spirit of thankfulness rather than expecting God to pay us back "ten times over" or "a hundredfold"—as some folks insist. We can never out-give God, of course, but neither does he *owe* us anything.

Prayer: *Father God, I confess I do envy—and maybe even resent—people who don't have to watch every penny. So help me concentrate on my family and look to you instead of wasting energy on envy. Thank you for your provision for us. Thank you for helping me provide for my children through new ways I haven't thought of yet.*

Thoughts to Ponder

1. What do you envy in other people?
2. What changes would you like to make in your financial situation?
3. What are you asking God to help you do?

Personal Ponderings

Be Financially Resolute

Make Rules and Keep Them

Day 29

Be pleased to save me, LORD; come quickly, LORD, to help me. Psalm 40:13

A radio program hosted by a respected Christian financial advisor offered four resolutions for financial stability:

- Use no credit cards
- Reduce existing debt
- Balance the checkbook each month to the penny
- Determine to conquer the biggest personal financial problem—whether that's overspending or impulse buying

To that list, I would add, Pray about every expense and allow the Lord to reveal creative ways to solve financial problems.

Granted, if we follow these suggestions, we have to analyze every purchase. And undoubtedly we'll have to say *no* often—to ourselves and to our children. Ah, don't we wish we had a dollar for every time we've heard, "But I *need* a new pair of jeans!"?

I loved buying clothes for my kids, but our budget wouldn't allow unplanned purchases. One thing that helped was to involve both teens in my check-writing sessions. In amazement, they'd watch the deposit decrease with each check written for house payment, utilities, grocery bills, car maintenance, and numerous piddling expenses.

Another friend decided on a more dramatic visual aid. She cashed her check for dollar bills, which she stacked in the middle of the table. She allowed her children to handle the dollars and exclaim, "Wow, we're rich!" Then as she read bills that needed to be paid, each child counted out the amount needed. Finally, only nine dollars were on the table, but three bills were still unpaid.

"What shall we do now?" she asked.

This wise mother had made her point and didn't have to use the visual aid again.

When we lived an hour north of New York City, my teens were surrounded by classmates whose fathers were CEOs of major companies. So to show them we weren't the only family having to watch our nickels and dimes, I'd pull rank every few weeks (mothers *are* allowed to do that) and plan a day trip to the city. We three would catch the Saturday southbound Metro North train, and Jay and I would marvel quietly at the interesting passengers and scenery along the Hudson River. At Grand Central Station, he and I enjoyed watching the people representing all social levels, from the Wall Street broker types to the ones panhandling for spare change. But Holly, my homebody, sighed often and felt I'd sentenced her to a day of dirt and noise.

Then one early December Saturday, a fur-coated matron got on the train with us and chirped to her preteen daughter for the entire trip about their planned Christmas shopping at several expensive shops.

As our train pulled into the 125th Street station, the stop just before Grand Central Station in the heart of one of New York City's most tired areas, the woman looked out the window at the decrepit apartment buildings and exclaimed, "Ugh! Why don't they move out of here?"

> *Debt is one sure way to have less than nothing!*

Holly turned to me, stunned at the woman's insensitivity to economic conditions. I nodded slightly, but the woman had made a point about materialism and poverty far better than I ever could have. Holly's attitude toward our days in New York City changed after that.

Those trips helped me too. Seeing the street panhandlers and families who were trapped in rundown neighborhoods kept me from giving in to the temptation to overuse credit cards. Even a little bit of debt can start a spiraling descent into financial chaos. Besides, debt is one sure way to have less than nothing!

We live in a society that equates success and blessing with money, so we American Christians often have a special problem in this area, especially since we want our children to fit in and have everything we didn't.

> *God promised to supply our needs, not our wants.*

But remember, God promised to supply our *needs*, not our *wants*, so discard the thought that if we're faithful to him, he's going to give us everything we desire. To insist he will discounts the faith of countless struggling Christians within the inner cities, in my beloved Kentucky mountains, and in developing countries around the world.

We don't have to have megabucks to meet our bills. Suggestions for creative ways to make extra money sometimes turn up in interesting places. I once found a trash-to-treasure magazine article alerting me to the possibility that the junky lamp in my hall closet was a collector's item worth $100. Before I read the article, I'd planned to sell the relic at our garage sale for $2!

Another idea that helped me was the Spare Change Drawer. Jay and Holly always needed a dollar or two for something at school, so I started tossing loose change and an occasional spare bill into a small dresser drawer every few days. Often, in addition to school needs, the drawer yielded enough quarters for a few gallons of gas or a trip to our favorite ice cream shop.

A second trove, the Gift Drawer, helped me when I needed a last-minute gift. Each time I found a sale table containing scented body wash or fun cookbooks, I'd buy them at the reduced price and stash them away to await an emergency gift need.

So don't despair. Pray, be creative, and take charge of your finances.

Prayer: *Father God, please help me stop worrying about our bills and, instead, start figuring out creative ways to pay them. Help me wisely consider every purchase. And help me stop envying what other people have.*

Thoughts to Ponder

1. What are your biggest financial challenges?
2. Are your children old enough to pressure you for things you can't afford? If so, how do you handle that? If not, how do you hope to face that time in the future?
3. What specific financial problem are you talking to God about?

Personal Ponderings

A Bare-Bones Christmas

And Other Joys

Praise be to God, who has not rejected my prayer or withheld his love from me! Psalm 66:20

Holiday gift-giving can throw another heavy ball in with the many already being juggled by single moms, can't it?

As our first Christmas in Colorado approached, I wondered how we were going to handle presents. The move had drained my financial resources, and my new job at an international ministry provided only a low-end salary.

I had learned long ago that the greatest gift we can give our children is a pleasant memory, so that Christmas I sighed, prayed, and then decided to concentrate on what truly is important about the season. And instead of lamenting what I had lost, I chose to rejoice in what I had left. After all, Jay and Holly don't remember the expensive toys that had been part of their earlier holidays, when we'd been a two-salaried family. But they do remember the first December when we were a family of three and impulsively donned snowsuits over our pajamas one midnight to make snow angels on the front lawn.

> *I had learned long ago that the greatest gift we can give our children is a pleasant memory.*

I thought of the coupon books they made when they were in elementary school. I still have the one Holly made for me when she was seven. In large, wobbly printing, she promised to help me with grocery shopping and dust the low parts of the tables. Maybe I'll redeem those coupons when I'm ninety. Thus, over dinner one night, the three of us agreed we'd devise creative coupons as our gifts to each other.

Amazingly, Christmas morning was fun! Jay gave Holly coupons for math help, and she promised to do several loads of his wash. One of Jay's gifts to me was a sheet of coupons for eight long walks—a sacrifice for my nonwalker! One of Holly's gifts was a free verse poem called "Parenting," in which she thanked me for being "a great person and mom."

Not having money forced us to think creatively.

Of course I cried when I read it. After all, many parents don't have things like that said about them until they're dead! Even now, I smile as I ponder how not having money forced us to think creatively.

A few hours after that morning's coupon exchange, four single parents and ten children from our new group of friends arrived for a potluck Christmas dinner. The adults and I had already agreed the only gifts we'd exchange would be acts of service or items we'd made. So when it was time to open gifts, we exchanged promises for help with cleaning, plates of cookies, and delightful homemade gifts, such as candlesticks made from gold-painted avocadoes. It was an incredible day—and all because we were determined not to let a lack of money spoil our fun.

But while my family and I found new and fun ways to celebrate Christmas, I later heard about mothers who were dealing with far greater issues than what the three of us faced. For Candace, gifts for her toddler daughter were the least of her worries when her husband demanded a divorce after their move to a new city for his job. Gloria and her two preteen children spent Christmas in a safe house until her widowed mother could arrange for their transportation to her home several states away. Petra's ex-husband

>

We were determined not to let a lack of money spoil our fun.

had their children for the holiday, so she spent the day praying as she took a long walk near her home. I'm grateful that, in time, all three families found ways to adjust to their new lives. And in time, they even found new ways to experience joy in the holiday, just as my children and I had done, and, I trust, you and your family are doing now.

So don't despair if you are forced to find new ways to celebrate this year. Pray, smile, be creative, and have fun!

Prayer: Father God, the term "new normal" is popular, and I'm trying to adjust to the life my children and I have now. This isn't what I planned, hoped for, prayed for. But this is what I have. So please help me find joyful moments in each day, especially during the holidays. And help me pour that joy into my children's lives as well.

Thoughts to Ponder

1. What's the toughest part of the holidays for you now?
2. What holiday traditions have you kept? Which ones are just memories?
3. What attitude adjustments have helped you the most?

Personal Ponderings

Day
31

Save Now for Retirement

It Arrives Sooner Than You Think

"I have told you these things, so that in me you may have peace. In this world you will have trouble. But take heart! I have overcome the world." John 16:33

Magazine articles and financial books give us hearty advice about investments, but most of us can't follow those tips because we're scrambling to buy groceries. We keep hoping we can save money "next year," but next year never seems to appear. Meanwhile, we find ourselves getting farther and farther down the road to retirement age.

This is another lesson I had to learn the hard way. So please hear me: You must put something away for your retirement, even if it's only a dollar a week in an account you never touch. I realize most banks require a minimum balance of a couple hundred dollars. But if you talk to an official, the rule can be bent for accounts that won't have withdrawals. Besides, something about seeing an account swell encourages us to save even more. And check out the pension savings plan at your work. For many of us that is the easiest way to save, since the money is taken out of our pay before we even see it.

While you consider minimum savings, take a financial inventory as you look at the amount of money you have coming in. Compare it to your expenses, including your home—whether rented or mortgaged—transportation costs, and normal bills for monthly needs.

Next, collect important papers such as insurance policies, bank account numbers, and mortgage lender or contact information for your landlord and put them in a large manila envelope labeled "Important Info."

Do you have a pension? List that contact as well. Some companies offer survivor benefits in addition to retirement payments.

> *If the unthinkable happened, who would raise your children?*

And speaking of survivor benefits, do you have a will? I don't like thinking about it, but single mothers die too. If the unthinkable happened, who would raise your children? Think you can't afford to have an official will prepared? Many law firms do *pro bono*, or free, work. So ask.

If you are horrified by what I've just said, look at it this way: Being prepared is like owning an umbrella. We may not need it, but it's nice to know we're ready for a storm.

Once you've started even a simple retirement account, taken financial inventory, and prepared a will, you can draw a deep breath.

Now it's time to teach your children about money—depending on their ages, of course.

Children need to be in charge of their own money, so even in their preteens, I gave Jay and Holly a small allowance. In turn, they were, on alternate days, expected to clear the dinner table and load the dishwasher, help with other household chores, and keep their own rooms neat. I accepted their differing definitions of "neat."

In addition, I kept a list of other jobs, such as sweeping out the garage, shoveling snow, and cleaning a closet, for which I'd pay extra. And, as a balance, I charged them when they missed the school bus and I had to taxi them to class. On some days I even warned them my schedule was so tight that if I had to drive them, the price would be $5. You ought to have seen those youngsters hurry out of their rooms then!

An important part of on-the-job training for your children is accepting their varying abilities. Jay would step over piles of laundry and claim he never saw them. But give him a room to paint, and he would finish the job quickly and well, especially if he could have the radio tuned to his favorite station.

An important part of on-the-job training for your children is accepting their varying abilities.

Holly, on the other hand, could not tolerate a mess. Even when it was her turn to cook, she cleaned as she went.

Maybe your children are opposites too. If so, you've probably already learned you'll drive yourself goofy if you expect the same results from different personalities. The important thing is to help them prepare for their future—just as you are preparing for your own.

Prayer: Father God, how am I supposed to plan for retirement and teach my children about money when I'm wondering how I'm going to pay this month's rent? Okay, I'll keep thinking about the practical financial steps I need to take, but you'll need to help me take that first step . . . and the next one . . . and the one after that.

Thoughts to Ponder

1. What's your greatest financial challenge right now?
2. What's your greatest fear for your financial future?
3. What good examples for saving money do you see around you? What bad ones?

Personal Ponderings

Day 32

Trust God for the Impossible
And Keep Good Financial Records

I am your servant; give me discernment that I may understand your statutes. Psalm 119:125

If you're highly organized you'll want to skip this section, because my annual tax preparation methods give logical minds headaches. But they work for me.

Throughout the year, I store all my receipts in the middle desk drawer. Then long about January 1, I start dreading sorting them into several piles. When I'm tired of dreading the chore, I finally declare an evening as tax night and sort everything into stacks: charity receipts, writing income, personal expenses, professional expenses, mortgage interest, and so on.

Then, once the receipts are organized, another evening is assigned to totaling the amounts and getting them ready for the tax preparer. If you are more organized than my pile system, you may want to invest in the computer software QuickBooks or Microsoft Excel. However you choose to handle your taxes, though, remind yourself of all you have conquered already. This is just one more hurdle you *can* sail over.

As I previously stated, the move to Colorado threw us into financial chaos at first. I prayed for help, then I started praying for a miracle. One morning I randomly thumbed through my Bible, not sure what I was looking for. Suddenly I stopped at chapter 20 in the book of Judges, which is the account of the Israelites asking the Lord if they were to fight the Benjamites. Twice he told them to fight. And twice they were soundly defeated, losing twenty-two thousand men the first day and eighteen thousand men the second day!

Not until the third battle did God give victory to the Israelites. Why had he wasted forty thousand men? At least in the book of Job, the reader knows that Job, a righteous man, suffered because of a conversation between Satan and God. But I found no such clue in the Judges 20 account. I was back to having to walk by blind faith, trusting that God *was* working even if I couldn't see the results.

That afternoon, a Monday, I pulled the last of my savings out to pay bills, bought groceries, and thanked the Lord we still had $34 to get us through the next month. I was calm. We could coast for four weeks. Then Jay came home from school.

The kitchen chair squeaked as I sat down. "Well, it's going to be interesting to see how the Lord works this out," I said.

"Mom, don't forget I need $70 for school fees by this Wednesday."

The kitchen chair squeaked as I sat down. "Well, it's going to be interesting to see how the Lord works this out," I said.

Holly strolled in then, so I had them both sit at the table with me.

I opened the checkbook. As I showed my teens the balance of $34, I said, "You know the prayer that went into our move. But if I've somehow missed the Lord's voice, then we're going to face some rough times until he chooses to take us through the problem. And if I haven't missed his voice, then I guess he's just trying to teach me something."

Both kiddos stared at the checkbook.

Jay spoke first. "No, I think God's trying to teach Holly and me to depend on him instead of on Good Ol' Mom."

I considered that before saying, "Maybe. But either way, we're starting an adventure. We're going to see God work in ways we would never have seen without this mess. And we may discover the joys of soup beans and cornbread, but God won't let us go hungry. My Kentucky days are going to pay off!"

> *"We may discover the joys of soup beans and cornbread, but God won't let us go hungry."*

Jay frowned at the mention of the beans. "That's carrying a good attitude too far, Mom."

I leaned forward. "And I'm telling you we're going to be all right," I said. "You just watch what the Lord is going to do. We can trust him to help us meet all the bills somehow."

I continued. "Remember the story of how England's George Müeller and the orphans he cared for sat at an *empty* table and thanked God for the food they were about to receive? And before they finished their prayer, a baker was at the door, saying he'd baked too many loaves of bread that morning, and could they use them? Or a milk wagon had broken down, and the driver didn't want to take the milk back to the dairy?

"Well, you just wait and see how the Lord takes care of your need for that $70."

Then we prayed, thanking the Lord for his future provision.

The next day's mail brought an unexpected utility bill—and a rebate check from Allied Van Lines for $254!

In the following weeks, we watched pennies like never before and continued to tithe. But that scary time certainly gave me a new understanding of the financial crises here in Colorado and across the nation during our recent recession. I also found the positive in being stone-cold broke: No one called with a sad story and a request for money.

Around that same time, Chris, a single mother in my Sunday school class, told about an unexpected bill for $117 marked "pay upon receipt." Her paycheck wasn't due until the end of the month, but instead of panicking, she gathered her three children for prayer and brainstorming. Her oldest daughter,

> *I also found the positive in being stone-cold broke: No one called with a sad story and a request for money.*

twelve, came up with the idea of a garage sale that coming weekend. With no time or money to put an ad in the paper, they prayed again—and then scoured closets and the garage for items they no longer used. Chris described the numerous cars that stopped at the sale, then dramatically asked, "Guess how much money we made that day? Exactly $117." What an answer to prayer! And what a faith-building lesson for her—and for her children.

So, single moms, let's try to be more faith-filled and creative than much of the world. After all, our heavenly Father is the God of the Impossible.

Prayer: Father God, I've had plenty of situations where I've been down to my last few dollars. But you didn't always show up in miraculous ways. Help me not to dwell on those former times but to keep trusting you in each present situation even as I ask for your help. Help me know your reality even when I don't see immediate results.

Thoughts to Ponder

1. How do you approach tax season each year?
2. Have you seen God work in impossible situations? If so, what happened? If not yet, what do you trust him to do now?
3. What have you learned about God and yourself during tough times?

Personal Ponderings

_____

_____

_____

Day 33

Angel Maids and Major Purchases
Preparation Beats Fear

Suppose one of you wants to build a tower. Will you first sit down and estimate the cost to see if you have enough money to complete it? Luke 14:28

I'm one of those people who never gets on a plane without looking for the location of the emergency exits. And when I check in to a hotel, I locate my floor's exit doors and stairs. Once

I've determined my way of escape, then I go about my normal, cheerful business.

Jay and Holly watched me do that for years, so when they were teens, and we were en route to visit relatives, they insisted I stop thinking the worst. I assured them I merely was being prepared just in case. But in our hotel one night, I gave in to their insistence, and didn't look for the stairs nearest our room.

To this day, we wonder if perhaps heaven hadn't been the scene of an angel alert.

You know what happened next, of course. Yep, early the next morning, the fire bell went off. For a startled moment, we looked at one another, not believing what we were hearing.

But I was the mother, so with seeming calmness I announced, "It's okay. Let's just get out of here."

I felt the door—no heat—and then opened it, and we stepped out into a pitch black hallway. Not even the usual emergency lights were visible.

"Father, help!" I implored.

Immediately, a woman's voice came out of the darkness.

"Is anyone on this floor?" she asked in a heavy Spanish accent.

"Three of us," I answered.

"Come this way," she said. "Follow my voice."

With Jay and Holly hanging on to my arms, I felt along the wall as we approached the woman. At last we saw her in a black-and-white maid's uniform, standing near the fire door.

I thanked her, but she waved us toward the stairs. "It's okay. But do hurry."

The fire quickly was contained, and we were able to return to our room to claim our luggage for checkout.

Amazingly, though, we didn't see that maid with the rest of the staff in the parking lot. And none of the other workers wore black-and-white uniforms. Isn't it interesting she appeared as soon as I asked our heavenly Father for help? To this day, we wonder if perhaps heaven hadn't been the scene of an angel alert.

We don't always receive such direct, on-the-spot answers to our petitions, of course. But every now and again, I'm convinced God *does* intervene directly through his messengers. So keep watching. You never know what form the miraculous will take.

By the way, Jay and Holly never teased me again about finding the exit locations.

Being prepared is part of my nature. In fact, that approach to life has helped me when I've had to make major purchases my family and I needed.

As a single mom, I've found two big headaches have been decisions over what to drive and where to live. And since I suspect these are probably problem areas for you too, let's take a look at what is involved in buying a car and buying or renting a house or apartment. Yes, if God provided an angel when we needed help in that hotel, cars and housing are no problem for him. But we have to do our part too. Let's look at car purchases first.

> *Keep watching. You never know what form the miraculous will take.*

Are you like me—bewildered by all things mechanical? Then let me encourage you: Don't despair. If I can jump over the car hurdle, you can!

First, the more you understand about your car, the less afraid you'll be and the less likely you'll be taken in by a not-so-honest mechanic. A good place to start learning is by reading the owner's manual that comes with the vehicle. I finally got around to reading the one that had been lying untouched in my glove compartment since Day One.

The best thing you can do to keep your car running smoothly for a long time is to have it maintained regularly. So ask your friends for recommendations of reputable repairmen.

But what if you have to buy another car?

I assume you are praying for our heavenly Father's help and trusting him to direct you to a good used car. Why should you consider a used car? Because it costs less than a new one.

Yes, some folks say when we buy a used car we may be buying someone else's problems. That's why a reputable mechanic is invaluable. Thus, before we buy a used car we need to make sure the seller will agree to our having it checked out by our chosen mechanic. That checkup may cost a few dollars, but it will be worth it in the long run.

Don't despair. If I can jump over the car hurdle, you can!

So where to start? If you don't have a specific make of car in mind and don't have the foggiest notion where to begin, just keep calm and do your homework. Sure, that's work, but we're used to hard work. After all, we're single moms!

Here are some tips:

Investigate Internet sites: Enter "sites for buying cars" in your Internet search engine. Several options will appear, including cars.com, edmunds.com, and valucar.com, along with local sites offering helpful information and specific advice for purchases.

Check out *Consumer Reports*. Visit the Consumer Reports.org website or thumb through *Consumer Reports Magazine* at your local library to see which cars have the best safety and maintenance records.

Call your insurance agent for a recommendation. Insurance can vary depending on a car's year, make, and model, so consider that cost before you start looking.

Look within your social group. Ask friends if they have or know of a reliable car for sale. Check the bulletin boards at work too.

Know how much you can afford. And once you've set that figure, don't allow yourself to be talked into spending just a little bit more. Those multiplied "little bits" can keep us bound by debt.

Ask questions. If you call about a car advertised by a private owner, here are a few suggested questions:

1. What's the general condition of the vehicle?
2. May I have my mechanic check it over?
3. Can the car pass the emissions test? (If the car can't pass the test in states where it's required, license plates won't be issued.)
4. Would you recommend this as a car for families with young children?

I've been pleased by sellers who've taken a deep breath and then answered honestly as they warned buyers not to buy their car because of potential problems.

Whew! You are halfway there. Next, we'll consider what to look for when you examine the car you are considering.

Take a deep breath. You *can* do this.

Prayer: Father God, being prepared "just in case" is an issue I need to work on. But thinking about car maintenance and purchase right now is exhausting. In time, I'll deal with that. Today, I trust you to help me with other details. Always, though, may I feel your presence and your peace. May my children and I experience your provision in new ways.

Thoughts to Ponder

1. Have you ever encountered one of God's messengers, either heavenly or earthly? If so, what happened? If not, are you open to watching for one? Why or why not?

2. What are your thoughts about the responsibilities that come with car ownership?

3. What have you found to be most helpful when you need to make a major purchase?

Personal Ponderings

_____

_____

_____

Day 34   # Confident Car Buying
Enjoy the Process

Whether you turn to the right or to the left, your ears will hear a voice behind you, saying, "This is the way; walk in it." Isaiah 30:21

You need a car and you've done your research. Now it's time to visit the car lots. As a rule, I've found most salespeople want to be helpful, so don't assume they are out to cheat potential customers. Besides, you've prayed and done your homework; you are ready.

I suggest you not buy the first vehicle you look at, if for no other reason than to satisfy your own future questions about what else might have been available. If the first car is exactly what you need and is within your price range, disregard the previous suggestion. But if you visit several lots, do take along a notebook to jot down important details: size of car, whether it's a 4- or 6-cylinder (the number of cylinders merely determines the power you'll have on the main roads), the general condition, and the price.

> *It's called a "test drive" because the customer is* testing *the brakes, steering, and general handling.*

When you find a car you like, ask to see the price stated in the Blue Book. This publication is produced by the National Automobile Dealers Association and properly is called the *NADA Official Used Car Guide*. Here you'll find information on the average trade-in value for specific cars, the retail price, and the amount of credit you can expect to receive. But remember, their listings are made up of averages. Thus, how much you pay for your particular car will depend on its condition, supply and demand, the locale, and the trade-in value of your present car, if you have one.

When I needed to buy a car, all I'd ever seen car customers do in movies was kick the tires—a sure sign of an amateur. So when my car's engine went out, I talked to anybody who was interested in cars, asked questions, and read several magazine articles. From that, I developed a mental list of what I needed: four doors, a big trunk, and enough engine power to keep my family safe.

Here are some things I learned to do:

- **Check the exterior.** Look for dents, rust, discolored paint, and welding ripples. Uneven paint or ripples in the metal are clues the car has been in an accident. That's especially important if the frame was bent. And deep rust means the car is rusting from the inside out, which could mean a major repair will arrive soon.

- **Check the interior.** Examine the controls—wipers, heat and air, turn signals, radio, and all lights. Look under the mats and loose carpet for rust. Look at the odometer to check the mileage, then look at the gas pedal. If the pedal is worn but the odometer shows low mileage or the numbers don't line up evenly, that's a pretty good sign the mileage has been rolled back.

- **Look under the hood.** Are the belts and hoses worn? Do any of the parts, such as the radiator or battery, show corrosion or rust?

- **Start the engine.** As the car idles, accelerate and listen for pings or knocks. That's a sign of potential problems. Let the car run for five minutes, then check under it for puddles. If they're greasy, you could be facing transmission problems.

- **Take the car for a drive.** It's called a "test drive" because the customer is *testing* the brakes, steering, and general handling.

- **Trust your instincts.** Listen for unusual noises when you shift, accelerate, or brake. Don't ignore any pulling or jerking.

See? It's not so scary when we know what we're looking for.

If, after looking at several used cars, you decide you want a new car after all and you plan to drive it forever—I've put more than 175,000 miles on my car in just a few years—you need to be aware of a few things.

It's not so scary when we know what we're looking for.

Don't splurge. Car dealers aren't in business for their health, so they're going to try to tack everything on to that new car they can. All the "bells and whistles" are nice conveniences but certainly not worth the cost for those of us who need to watch dollars and pennies! So just stay with the essentials.

Do negotiate. You aren't buying a loaf of bread with a fixed price. You're trying to get your best price on something that can be purchased for less than the sticker price. So go for it.

> Do negotiate. *You aren't buying a loaf of bread with a fixed price.*

Ask questions. And don't be timid about asking for sufficient information on those expensive extras. When I bought my first car, the young salesman tried to sell me a fabric protector package for several hundred dollars.

I quietly asked, "What does that package do?"

He gave me an elaborate song-and-dance about the importance of protecting the car's interior from spills.

So I gave him the look I used to give students who thought they were putting one over on "Old Lady Aldrich" and asked the question again. "But what does the package actually do?"

He blushed, then stammered, "Buy a can of fabric protector and spray the seats."

I did exactly that.

Congratulations, you've conquered the car hurdle. Now you'll set up a regular schedule for basic maintenance, such as oil changes and tire rotation. And you'll be prepared for your area's storms. Here in Colorado, our sudden spring storms can dump up to a foot of snow within a few hours. So we keep emergency kits in our vehicles' trunks. Most of us carry a bag of cat litter for traction, a first aid kit, a flashlight and flashers, booster cables, road maps—if we don't have a GPS—basic tools, a can of instant flat-fixer, ice scrapers, a folding shovel, and a pair of old boots.

The National Weather Service says I also should have a blanket or sleeping bag, foil-wrapped matches, candles, paper towels, an extra coat, socks and gloves, nonperishable food such as peanut butter and raisins, a compass, and a pocket knife.

Okay, I confess. That's next week's car project.

Prayer: Father God, this sounds so easy. But I'm still nervous about making a mistake. So I'm going to trust your promise in Isaiah 30:21 to guide me. And I need that moment-by-moment guidance in more than just a potential vehicle purchase. Help me listen for your voice and your guidance in every decision I make. And help me not be afraid.

Thoughts to Ponder

1. Are you comfortable making major purchases alone? Why or why not?
2. What's the largest purchase you've ever made? What happened?
3. What advice do you have for other single mothers making a first-time major purchase alone?

Personal Ponderings

Housing Decisions

No Need to Panic

I am poor and needy; may the Lord think of me. You are my help and my deliverer; you are my God, do not delay.
Psalm 40:17

Has your single-mother status forced you into a new housing situation? Are you concerned your children will be adversely affected if you have to downsize living space for a while? Let me encourage you: Yes, make sure your family is safe, but remember that your children will carry memories of your love into their adulthood. And those memories outshine housing.

In fact, I remember a woman who recalled her childhood on a Louisiana bayou houseboat.

"That was the only place my mother could afford," she said. "But I never understood her embarrassment about our living arrangements. I loved every minute there with her and often wish I could go back to those days."

So take a deep breath and straighten your shoulders. You *can* handle housing decisions—just as you've handled so many other decisions. Of course, the most important first step is prayer. But even with prayer, you still have plenty of practical things to consider.

Here are some tips for buying a house:

Investigate Internet sites: As with your car research, enter "sites for buying houses" in your Internet search engine. Several national and local options will appear, including homes.com and homefinder.com, offering advice and potential locations.

Talk to others: Call school administrators, pastors, and anyone else in your chosen area who might be able to answer your questions.

Choose your Realtor. Work with someone from a reputable firm. That professional can answer your questions as well as give you a list of mortgage companies and make arrangements for all inspections.

Investigate a too-good-to-be-true deal. Some homes, for instance, may have a leaky basement that shows up only after a heavy storm. Others can't pass a radon inspection for natural radioactive gases, so the owners are willing to sell at a ridiculous price.

Check for cracks over inside doors. Defects may mean the foundation has shifted.

Check the driveway for cracks. Deep ones may signal underground problems. For example, parts of our city are located over old mines, which have the potential for collapsing tunnels.

Check for a sagging roof. If evident, you may face a serious foundation problem.

Check the water pressure. Turn on the tap and then flush the toilet. The water flow in the tap should remain unchanged.

Ask to review utility bills for the past year. If they're unusually high, the house may have poor insulation.

Ask about the furnace and air-conditioning units. Ask how old they are and when they were last cleaned and inspected.

Don't assume anything. For instance, ask which appliances stay with the house or apartment and if they are in good working order.

Insist on a structural inspection. Once you've found a potential new home, no matter how your own inspection went, take a deep breath. When we're under pressure, we often lean on our emotional reactions to the property. That can be valid, but an official inspection will reveal the condition of the house and its foundation. Yes, it may cost a couple hundred dollars, but you'll know what you're getting. That information will save you from an unpleasant surprise later.

There! That's enough to get you started. The Internet, library, or your realty office will have more details to help you feel confident about your purchase.

But what if you need to rent? You may have read this far and decided that buying a house is out of the question. Maybe you've studied your financial situation and realize you're doing well just to meet current bills.

When we're under pressure, we often lean on our emotional reactions to the property.

Finding a decent rental when you're a single mom with limited means is not easy, especially since many landlords insist, "No pets, no children." But this is not impossible, so after you've prayed, here are some ways to get started.

Find out what's available. Who does rent to single-parent families with children—with or without pets? Talk with others in your situation. Read the classifieds closely. Make inquiries.

Now, let's assume you've found an affordable place that accepts children. Great, you're all set. But what if it's going to take two incomes to swing it? Then let's look at this next suggestion.

Team up with another single mother. Have you found a nice place but it's too expensive for one income? Or are you a divorced or widowed mother who's stuck with a house you can't afford to keep by yourself? Either way, search for another single mom to share costs and responsibilities. Advertise through your church, your workplace, the local supermarket bulletin board, or the classifieds. But as you receive responses, make sure you talk through—and put into writing—every detail of your expectations and hers. Again, assume nothing.

Consider mobile home living. Check out mobile home parks in your area. As a rule, whether you rent or buy, mobile homes cost less than conventional housing of comparable size. Not sure about the area? Ask the police. They'll answer your questions.

Consider subsidized housing. Federally subsidized housing is available in some areas for mothers and children with limited income. Such accommodation is a boon for the working mother who can manage a month's rent but can't come up with a security deposit and first- and last-month's rents at the same time. Check with your local Department of Housing and Urban Development to determine if you're eligible for their program. Even if you have to go on a waiting list, it's worth the wait.

> *Not sure about the area? Ask the police. They'll answer your questions.*

Remember the Louisiana woman who spent her childhood on a bayou houseboat? Just as her mother, though unknowingly, created wonderful memories, you can as well. The texture of the walls doesn't mean as much as your love that surrounds your children.

Prayer: Father God, I'm grateful I can trust you to guide me step-by-step. Thank you that, even if I start to panic about all the decisions I must make, you are just a whisper away.

Thoughts to Ponder

1. What's your present housing situation? Do you need to change it? Why or why not?
2. What's your major concern about housing for your family?
3. Were any of these suggestions new to you? If so, which ones? If not, what previous experiences helped?

Personal Ponderings

Pondering
Parental Goals

Planning the Right Path

Do not merely listen to the word, and so deceive yourselves.
Do what it says. James 1:22

Why can't our children do what they're supposed to? Why can't they immediately complete assigned tasks? Why can't they be perfect?

For the same reason we can't be perfect: We all are human beings and not angelic creatures. Besides, our children are *children*.

We've read enough advice from experts to know solid parental goals include teaching children self-control and acceptable behavior. We know we should be consistent, make clear rules, criticize constructively, act promptly, and issue reasonable punishment.

And I suppose we're to do all that without yelling.

Yes, we know the basics of good parenting. So why do we moms struggle? I'm convinced it's because we often are so intent on our own challenges that we merely *react* to our children instead of *responding*. And we're so busy juggling our many responsibilities that we often don't see the problems until they become crises. One tired mother told me she'd always thought children were like weeds—if she kept them fed and watered, they'd just naturally grow. Too late, she discovered raising children takes prayer, involvement, and thoughtful planning.

We understand prayer's importance and we try to be involved in our children's activities, but what's the planning piece? Remember Alice in *Alice in Wonderland* asking the Cheshire Cat for directions?

"That depends a good deal on where you want to get to," said the Cat.

"I don't much care where—" said Alice.

"Then it doesn't matter which way you go," said the Cat.

Unlike Alice, we parents do care and know in general where we want to go—and where we want our children to go. But let's be more specific. I'm a list maker, so even as I prayed for Jay and Holly, I made a list of qualities I wanted them to develop. Here are the first five from that list:

1. Build a close relationship with the heavenly Father.
2. Develop spiritual discernment in making decisions.
3. Learn to have a balanced view of money.
4. Possess a compassionate heart that responds wisely to true needs.
5. Allow themselves to bounce back from a mistake but learn from the experience.

Did my children always display evidence of what I was trying to teach? Of course not. But my conscious effort helped them understand some of the challenges awaiting them in adulthood, and my list helped me be more consistent in my parenting. Along the way, I also outlined my own single-parenting priorities. These values headed my list:

God

Jay and Holly

Work

Extended family

Friends

By the way, as I considered my constant juggling of family and work at an international ministry, I often reminded myself that if I sacrificed my children for the sake of "God's work," it was no longer God's work. But back to setting goals for ourselves and our children: Once I determined the qualities I wanted my children to develop, I contemplated specific parenting guidelines I needed to develop. Did those guidelines include rules? Of course.

> *Yes, teens may howl when it comes to following rules, but they gain a sense of security if they know the limits.*

Yes, teens may howl when it comes to following rules, but they gain a sense of security if they know the limits. We parents need to communicate our expectations clearly. Teens don't like hearing "You should have known better" any more than we do.

Along with handing out rules—even good ones—we need to add encouragement. An occasional "You're doing a great job" or "I'm proud of you" carries power. After all, if children feel good about themselves, they will be better equipped to resist having to prove their worth through dangerous or inappropriate actions. So help your children find something at which they can excel. By developing positive skills, not only is the child's self-esteem bolstered, but he or she isn't left with great blocks of unclaimed time. The adage "Idle hands are the devil's workshop" is true.

One of my greatest struggles as I helped my children find activities suited to their interests and skill level was allowing them to venture beyond my watchful control. I had tons of fears about the world outside our home, so I wanted to keep my kids under my wing. But I've grown only when I was allowed to take responsibility, so I figured that was the only way my children were going to grow too. The process, however, had to be exactly that—a process. The bird realm offers a good example: Mother birds don't push their little ones from the nest and expect them to fly immediately. Instead, they lead them onto the limb next to the nest, then nudge them to hop along the limb for a while. Next come little flight loops around the tree. In the same way, we need to give our children little loops of responsibility under our loving watch as we prepare them for greater responsibilities in the world beyond our home tree.

If children feel good about themselves, they will be better equipped to resist having to prove their worth through dangerous or inappropriate actions.

Believe me, those little flight loops and prayerful goals pay big dividends later.

Prayer: Father God, I confess I identify with that mother who thought children are like weeds, needing only to be fed and watered to grow. I feel inadequate to guide my kiddos toward responsible adulthood, especially when they are so young now. But I know I have to start sometime. So please guide me as I define what I want for the little ones you have given me. Please guide me as I define specific goals, first for myself and then for my children.

Thoughts to Ponder

1. What specific qualities do you want your children to develop?
2. What are your specific single-parenting priorities?
3. In what ways can you provide "little loops around the tree" as you teach your children responsibility?

Personal Ponderings

Peer Pressure

Day 37

Provide Broad Shoulders

Be joyful in hope, patient in affliction, faithful in prayer.
Romans 12:12

Are your children old enough to encounter peer pressure? If not, take a deep breath and rejoice. But sooner or later, this challenge will be a reality. So plan now how you will help them face it later.

If your children are facing peer pressure now, take two deep breaths and pray. But don't despair. Yes, this time can be so intense that some kids may break rules and even make unfortunate choices. These infractions may not be acts of deliberate disobedience but the youngster's inability to stand alone against peers. At such times, our kids need our help, not our rejection.

> *"Let me help you carry your challenges until you're strong enough to carry them alone."*

Do you remember the challenges you faced as a teen? Oh, I remember mine! So as Jay and Holly approached middle school years, I told them, "When you're in a tough situation and you don't want the others to mock your decision, blame me. Just say, I can't. My mom would ground me for life. You've seen her; you know she will."

Then I added, "Let me help you carry your challenges until you're strong enough to carry them alone."

In those early years, I was relieved to occasionally overhear either Jay or Holly say into the phone, "I can't. My mom would ground me for life," even though I had no idea what they were being asked.

I'd always stroll past them as though I was stone deaf. But inside I rejoiced.

Even though I tried to protect my children, I also didn't isolate them. So I encouraged them to invite their friends over on weekends. (Okay, so I wanted to know where they were and what they were doing!) I supplied the pizza, cheese and crackers, fruit and dip, and brownies. My teens knew the rules: They could invite whomever they wanted, but no one was allowed to drink, smoke, swear, or watch inappropriate movies in our home.

Admittedly, both kids occasionally invited friends who made me a little nervous, but I still welcomed them warmly. For many, this was a haven, and perhaps my rules gave them an idea of what structured family life looks like.

I didn't invade the group, but I always "just happened" to be baking, the results of which were served fresh out of the oven as the teens strolled in on Friday evenings. Of course, then I was within earshot as I cleaned up the kitchen while they watched a movie.

Only once did we have a problem. Holly had attended the school basketball game with a group of friends. I knew the driver was responsible, so I allowed her to go, and then invited the whole gang back for pizza. I hadn't stressed they were to watch a movie from our collection, so one of the guys brought his favorite.

> *Then in the midst of my wimpy decision-making process,* **the** *swear word came tearing out of the screen.*

Shortly after the movie started, I strolled through the family room on my way to the laundry room. (I always made sure I needed to get towels from the dryer.) The sound of gunshots and shouting let me know this was a film I'd rather they not watch. Still, I hesitated to shut it off, not wanting to cause a scene.

Then in the midst of my wimpy decision-making process, *the* swear word came tearing out of the screen. Not only had I heard it, but the kids knew I'd heard it.

With the others looking out the corners of their eyes at me, I motioned for Holly to join me in the living room. Her "uh-oh" merely increased the tension.

She followed me. "Well, Holly, you know the movie is going to be turned off," I said. "Now, would you like *me* to do that or would you rather take care of it yourself?"

Her eyes widened. Trying to save herself embarrassment, she muttered, "Mom! Like I don't hear that word, and worse, at school."

"Unfortunately, you do," I answered. "But this is not school. This is our home. And you are not going to hear that word within these walls. Now, again I ask: Do you want me to turn it off or are you going to take care of it?"

She huffed. "You really are treating me like a baby."

She said it in such an uncharacteristically bratty way I easily could have overreacted. Instead, I had the good sense to wrap her in a bear hug.

"No, I'm treating you with the respect you deserve, which is exactly the way I expect your friends to treat you," I said. "If I thought you were a baby I would have thundered in there and turned it off myself. Out of respect for your maturity, I'm giving you the choice."

She went back into the family room and muttered, "Sorry, guys. My mom says we can't watch this."

I expected to hear groans from the group. Instead, two of the boys quickly apologized. "Oh, Holly, we're sorry. We didn't mean to get you in trouble."

"I'm not in trouble. We just can't watch this."

Whew. Another battle won. So, yes, give your children love, guidelines, rules—and a strong shoulder to lean on.

Prayer: Father God, I remember the challenges I faced in my own growing-up years. Too often it was tempting to think nobody cared and follow the crowd. But even as I confess that, I am aware today's youngsters face situations beyond anything I experienced. Back then I didn't know about the Internet and had never heard about "selfies" or social media bullying. I have two choices now: I can panic or I can ask for your help as I guide my children through the days ahead. I gratefully choose your strength.

Thoughts to Ponder

1. What peer pressure did you face as a teen? How did you handle it?
2. Of all the pressures you anticipate your children will face, which ones concern you the most?

3. What steps are you taking now to help your children resist peer pressure later?

Personal Ponderings

Day 38

Consequences and Other Joys

We Are the Parents

Teach me to do your will, for you are my God; may your good Spirit lead me on level ground. Psalm 143:10

Most of us have read the tough-love books telling us we must let our children experience the consequences of their actions. Those lessons are tough for both the parent watching the event and the child experiencing it. But for many of us, that's the only way we learned important lessons. Our children are no different.

Ginny had to bite her lip while her son spent his allowance unwisely. Then, because she refused to advance more funds, he had to forego other activities. She knew she was teaching him long-range lessons, but it still was difficult to watch him miss fun with his friends.

She could have rationalized giving him the extra spending money, especially since he had "already lost so much in life." But she wisely chose to have them both tough it out so he would learn to budget his money better. It took a few rough weeks, but when he saw that his sorrowful eyes and "just this once" pleas weren't working, he started watching his money more closely.

And I had to let Jay go to school without lunch several times as we were both withdrawing from those Good-Ol'-Mom-will-come-through habits. When he was in elementary school, I'd often take his forgotten lunch to him. But when we moved to New York at the beginning of his eighth-grade year, we agreed I wouldn't haul his lunch to school anymore. After our deal, I found his lunch in the refrigerator after he'd already boarded the school bus only three or four times. Of course, he'd eat as soon as he got home at three o'clock, so I knew his health wasn't in jeopardy. Within a couple of weeks, he no longer forgot his lunch. Problem solved.

Then the day came when I opened the refrigerator to get my lunch for work and discovered Holly had forgotten hers. Was it fair to treat her with tough love the first time she failed? But if I gave in, wouldn't I be teaching her she didn't have to worry? That Good Ol' Mom would swoop in to rescue her?

I stood in front of the open refrigerator for several moments, arguing with myself. Finally I decided if this became a habit, we'd deal with it then. I picked up her lunch bag and headed to her school. As I drove, I mentally argued with the tough-love experts, deciding Holly wasn't a candidate for their techniques just yet. Besides, I was going to suffer more than she would if I left her lunch in the refrigerator.

I arrived at school a few minutes before her first class began. She and several of her friends were still by their lockers, combing their hair and chatting about the day's plans. Holly turned as I approached. The look of surprise and pleasure on her face made the trip worth it. She thanked me profusely for bringing her lunch, reminding me she'd made egg salad and had been disappointed to discover she'd left it home.

> *I was going to suffer more than she would if I left her lunch in the refrigerator.*

Our long-standing custom has been to hug good-bye, but after I handed her the lunch and heard one more thank-you, I stood there awkwardly for a moment. I wanted that hug, but I didn't want to embarrass her in front of her friends.

Finally I said, "Well, I've got to head to work. Who wants a hug before I go?"

Kristi hopped up from the floor. "I do!"

I gave her a motherly bear hug, while Holly stood by, red-faced and saying, "Mom!"

Then Jessica said, "Me too." One by one, I gave her five friends a squeeze to send them into the day. Finally only Holly was left. I hugged her and hurried out the door.

That night, as we cleared the table after dinner, she again thanked me for taking her lunch to school. I said I hoped I hadn't embarrassed her by hugging her friends.

She shrugged. "Well, you did at first because you're always doing weird things. But later, the girls said you're pretty neat. I just agreed with them."

I gave her another big hug right then.

By the way, that was the only time she forgot her lunch.

While it's wonderful to be understanding, forgiving, and open to discussing house rules, the time will come when you have to make a decision—and not let yourself be talked out of it. When those moments came for us, Jay and Holly tried to argue.

But I'd say, "Just write this on your list of Rotten Things My Mom Used to Do. I'll sign it so you have proof when you show it to some future psychologist."

The argument always ended there.

Then came the year I decided we were going to attend an honest-to-goodness Fourth of July fireworks display. In the past, we'd always been at our lake trailer, and the kiddos had been content with sparklers. But this time I wanted to show them a sky filled with orange and green and red and blue. Okay, so *I* wanted to see a display again.

> *"Just write this on your list of Rotten Things My Mom Used to Do. I'll sign it so you have proof when you show it to some future psychologist."*

When I excitedly told them about my plans, they just glanced at each other with a here-we-go-again look. That afternoon, however, ten-year-old Jay ran into the house with his own news. "Mom! Timmy's got a bag of bottle rockets we're gonna shoot off tonight. Isn't that great?!"

I looked up from my mending. "Remember? We're going to the park to see fireworks."

Jay frowned. "I don't wanna go. I wanna shoot bottle rockets."

For several minutes, I tried to reason with him.

Finally I said, "That's enough. I'm pulling rank. You *are* going to the fireworks."

Jay glared at me before stomping to his room.

All through dinner, he was sullen. When we arrived at the park, he ignored my attempts to draw him into the conversation Holly and I were enjoying.

I opened the cooler. "What do you want? Juice or cola?" I thought he'd refuse.

Instead he mumbled, "Cola."

I bit the inside of my lip to keep from commenting.

Finally I said, "That's enough. I'm pulling rank. You are going to the fireworks."

At last, the smoke rocket went up to test the degree of darkness. It was followed by an explosion that filled the sky with a brilliant orange umbrella. Green spinners followed, then red and white arches.

As the crowd emitted a collective "ahhhh," Jay turned to me, his eyes sparkling. "Wow, Mom. This is great!"

My wink was the closest I came to saying, "I told you so."

Prayer: Father God, why is good parenting so difficult? When our children are born, the hospital staff hands us a precious little bundle and tells us to go home and enjoy. They don't tell us about sleepless nights and colic and arguments and worry. And this business about tough love is difficult to enforce and difficult to watch. Is that how you feel when you watch us suffer the consequences of our actions? Do you sigh when we yell at you? Do you weep when we refuse the blessings you want to give us?

Thoughts to Ponder

1. What are your thoughts about children dealing with the consequences of their actions?
2. Are you ever tempted to do for your children what they should do for themselves? Why or why not?
3. Have your children ever argued against an activity but later were glad they participated? If so, what was the event? If not, how did you avoid a potential argument?

Personal Ponderings

Day
39

Discipline, Not Abuse

Teaching Responsibility

No discipline seems pleasant at the time, but painful. Later
on, however, it produces a harvest of righteousness and peace
for those who have been trained by it. Hebrews 12:11

Counselors and child experts remind us that children who have
time on their hands aren't happy. In fact, those who have no
chores and no responsibilities tend to quarrel much more
than those who have to be busy around the home.

Still, we single mothers easily can get trapped into thinking
we have to juggle *every* ball attached to everything needing to be
accomplished. Here's good news: The one labeled "chores" easily can be passed along to the children. But we need to remember
we will have fewer discipline problems when we make sure the
kiddos understand exactly what we expect from them when we
assign chores.

Usually we *can't* just say, "Clean your room." We have to be specific: "Make your bed. Hang up your clothes. Put away the toys. Dust the dresser, chair, and desk."

I reminded myself of that fact many times when I sent Jay back to his room with the instruction he was to look at the mess through *my* eyes. Let's face it: Most teen boys don't share their mother's obsession with neatness. I had to learn that Jay's room was Jay's room.

My kiddos liked having a chore list on the kitchen counter so they could cross off each item as they finished. I found a list worked better than just giving them another assignment after they'd finish the first one. If they kept getting a string of chores, they'd be defeated, thinking the work would never end. We all need to see that the end goal is possible.

I also found they worked best if I worked with them. So when they first were learning to work, I couldn't just say, "Put all your toys on the shelf." I needed to say, "*Let's* put all your toys on the shelf."

Even young children can be in charge of an occasional meal that doesn't require cooking. There's nothing wrong with cold chicken sandwiches for dinner. The important thing is that we are spending time together and talking about our day. Meals together often can be the family's cement.

With my entry into single parenting, I didn't cook the way I used to—meat and potatoes on the table every night at 5:30 p.m.—but I also refused to give in to the fast-food syndrome. Our meals consisted of a protein and a crunchy vegetable. I also made double portions so the leftovers could provide another meal. On those nights, all we had to add was a fresh salad.

One of our standard dinners each week was baked chicken. Not only did we get a good meal, but the leftovers provided several lunches throughout the week. That was a boon since I refuse to buy regular lunchmeat. It's too expensive and filled with salt and nitrites.

Some good things came out of my busy schedule: Jay and Holly had to take more responsibility in the kitchen. The best system we found was for them to help me cook dinner and clean up the kitchen afterward on alternate days.

Those first meals the kiddos put together were interesting. Holly enjoyed trying cookbook recipes and trading ideas with her friends, while Jay served whatever was in the refrigerator. But he soon progressed from warmed-over pizza to spicy potatoes and a marvelous cheese-broccoli soup. Today, he often prepares a company dinner complete with marinated meat, homemade bread, and his personalized chocolate dessert cups filled with black raspberry mousse. Ah, another victory.

> *We need to be attentive to our children's varying abilities instead of expecting perfection right away.*

But even as we parents persevere, we need to be attentive to our children's varying abilities instead of expecting perfection right away.

Proverbs 22:6 says, "Start children off on the way they should go, and even when they are old they will not turn from it." Several biblical scholars insist the original meaning is, "start off a child in *his* way." In other words, we are to help our children discover their strengths and how to best use them. Undoubtedly, you already are aware that what works for one won't work for another. For example, what is effective discipline for one child often doesn't even faze his or her sibling. What an awesome responsibility we have to help our children discover their separate strengths.

Yes, that discipline includes rewards for good choices and consequences for bad ones. While we're on the topic of discipline, let's talk about spanking. Sadly, child abuse is a problem in our society. Whenever the statistics are cited, these same reasons for the parents' abusive behavior come up—stress, increased pressures, unrealistic expectations, frustration at the way life has turned out, alcohol or drug abuse, lack of an extended family support system, or a continuing cycle of abuse from generation to generation. And the potential for abuse often is especially real for single mothers who are juggling too many responsibilities alone. Think about that: Little children are being hurt by the one person they are looking to for protection.

When I was overly tired or worried about bills or being pulled in too many directions, nothing was right. But I learned to say, "I can't handle this well right now," and withdraw until I could cool down. And while I cooled down, I talked to the Lord. Once I had cooled down, I could tackle the issue in a calmer way. Remember, children don't read minds any more than we do, so they aren't going to know they are loved unless they experience it through words and action.

Discipline includes rewards for good choices and consequences for bad ones.

By the way, whatever your thoughts are about spanking, I'll say this: Don't spank your children when you are angry. Instead, try what I call the BWAL minute: Breathe, warn, act, love. Taking a breath reminds us the goal is to correct wrong behavior, not strike out in anger. The warning gives the child the opportunity to make a better choice. The action part that I like is to have the child retreat to another room or specific chair to think about his or her wrong decisions. One young friend assigns her sons a specific number of minutes in the Thinking Chair based on their ages. Thus, the five-year-old has to think about his offense for five minutes. (I wish I'd been that creative at her age!) After the allotted minutes, the love part comes in as she asks her child to explain what would be more appropriate action. Then she affirms her love.

If you rolled your eyes at the above account and feel a spanking is in order, smack the child's bottom—never that little face.

For those times when you are dealing with wearying, repeated action, try telling your children what you need from them and what you're willing to offer in return. Sometimes that translates into, "When I get home from work, I need to at least get my coat hung up before you spring the latest crisis on me. Give me a few minutes, and I'll be ready to listen then."

If you realize you need help beyond my suggestions, input "prevent child abuse" into your computer's search engine for a long list of local, regional, and national agencies. If you don't have a computer, your local library may have social services pamphlets listing anonymous hotline numbers. The important thing is that your precious children be protected. You may be all they have.

Prayer: Father God, how do I even begin to pray about discipline? Too often I punish instead of instruct. And too often I punish in anger. This is too much for me, but it's not too much for you. So please, please help me respond as you want me to. Help me not ignore wrong choices or overreact to typical childish action. Help me show my love—and yours—to my children.

Thoughts to Ponder

1. What do you think of when you hear the word *discipline*?
2. What is your early experience with discipline?
3. What are your present discipline challenges? Your victories?

Personal Ponderings

The Impossible Task

Day 40

Trying to Please Everyone

Remember your word to your servant, for you have given me hope. My comfort in my suffering is this: Your promise preserves my life. Psalm 119:49–50

When I entered single parenting, it seemed as though every friend and relative lined up to give me suggestions/advice/orders about how to raise my children.

Do the people around you offer unsolicited opinions too? If so, these are the times we express our appreciation for their concern—no need for a big argument—and go on about our business. After all, we love our relatives and friends, but we are the ones raising our children.

Do you need encouragement about how useless it is to follow the advice of others? Then allow me to retell a shortened version of Aesop's fable about a man caught in a similar situation:

The man and his son were on their way to market, leading their donkey and enjoying the day.

One of their neighbors saw them and said, "Now, isn't that silly? You have a fine donkey, but both of you are walking."

So the father set his son on the donkey, and they continued toward the market.

But after a few minutes, another friend saw them and said to the son, "How rude you are to ride while your old father must walk."

So the father joined the child on the donkey's back. It wasn't long, though, until they passed a third friend.

"How thoughtless you are," he said, "to make this poor donkey carry both of you."

So they slid off the donkey, and the strong father promptly picked up the animal and put it across his shoulders.

As they slowly walked along, a fourth neighbor saw them. "Well, that's the most stupid thing I've ever seen. Donkeys are supposed to be ridden, not carried."

See? We can't please everyone. So let's apply that same philosophy to our parenting.

When I made the decision not to remarry despite the comments and attempted setups by relatives, my choice meant I was determined to raise Jay and Holly alone. Again, my decision ran contrary to the expectations of my relatives, especially my dad.

A typical Kentuckian, Dad was a teller of tales, and most of his accounts of life in the Appalachian Mountains were filled with high drama. I grew up listening, horrified and in tears, to epics of a neighbor murdering his wife, of children being given away, or of fires consuming wooden houses within minutes.

We can't please everyone. So let's apply that same philosophy to our parenting.

But the story he told of an ancestor's refusal to accept his second wife's children always stirred my temper rather than my tears.

The relative's first wife had died, leaving him with three youngsters. Grief and reality often walked together in those mountains at the turn of the nineteenth century, so within a matter of weeks, he was looking for another wife to care for his children. The prime candidate was a widow with three young boys. They married quickly, and the woman's sons were sent to live with their uncle in a neighboring town.

When the mule-drawn wagon with the three boys in it started down the lane away from the only house they knew as home, the youngest began to scream, "Mama! Mama!"

When Dad reported the child's grief at being separated from his mother, I reacted.

"How could she give up her children like that?"

"What do you mean?" Dad asked. "The house was too small for three more boys."

"But not too small for the ones she later had with her new husband. I'd be cussed before I'd give up my children like that!"

"What would you do?" Dad would say. "There you are stuck with no means of support for yourself or your youngsters. You'd be living off other people's charity."

At seventeen, I had more fight than sense. But I also had mother bear instincts, and I knew even then I'd fight for my cubs.

"We'd walk to the nearest town even if it took days," I said. "I'd find work or I'd walk the streets and beg, but I'd feed my children. And no man on this earth would take 'em from me! She was spineless for giving hers up, and he was scum for making her do so!"

Neither of us ever won over the other when it came to airing our views on those ancestors. In fact, that argument between Dad and me was two decades old when I became a single parent. Suddenly, though, my dad took comfort in my long-standing position. He knew I would take good care of my children—his grandchildren—and no one could ever make me give them up. And he was right!

Yes, relatives expect us to act a certain way, but they often dump their expectations onto our children as well. In fact, after my husband's funeral, his dad did that as he said good-bye in our kitchen.

As my father-in-law hugged ten-year-old Jay, he said, "Take care of your mother. You're the man of the house now."

I was standing where I could see Jay's face, and I was struck by the panic that flashed across his eyes.

I looked at my son's grandfather. "No. Jay is the ten-year-old *son* in this house."

Jay has since commented on how much it meant to him I'd say that. He'd just lost one parent; he needed the security of knowing his mom was in charge.

After Karen became single again, her former father-in-law complained about her keeping the two children in a Christian school and, as he said, "shielding them from the real world."

Karen was convinced the school was best for the children for the present since it provided stability. So like Hannah in 1 Samuel 1:15 when the priest Eli accused her of being drunk, Karen quietly answered the charges:

He'd just lost one parent; he needed the security of knowing his mom was in charge.

"I appreciate your concerns," she said. "But I'm the one who's responsible for the children. I'm the one who must stand before God and give an account."

Even though Karen calmly and respectfully had answered the accusation, she later shared the conversation with a trusted friend. "It's a bigger issue than just the public or private school matter," she said through tears. "It's whether I know what's best for *my* children."

I can identify with that feeling because some relatives voiced strong opinions when I accepted an editorial job just north of New York City. They'd never been there themselves; they had seen the city only in movies. But they insisted we were moving to one of the world's roughest spots.

As it turned out, only the financial part was rough. I loved the cloistering tree branches that hung over the road near my office and the gentle rolling hills that reminded me of my own beloved Kentucky. And I especially was pleased with the schools. So I shrugged off the comments. By the time I'd decided to move away, I'd stopped trying to please the relatives.

I wish I'd had Amy's creativity that first year of single parenting when I was trying to deal with raw emotions and juggle new responsibilities while facing the relatives' demands. Rather than dwelling on the notions of what others thought she should do, Amy would read her personal list of the kind of mom she could be, given her circumstances and the needs of her child, and then remind herself of what God had called her to. That plan certainly was far better than trying to fit the impossible standards of people around her. I'm convinced making—and reading often—a list like that is a perfect way to face each new day and each new challenge.

"I'm the one who's responsible for the children. I'm the one who must stand before God and give an account."

Instead of coming up with a creative list like Amy's, though, one day I poured out my frustration to longtime friends Dan and Janet. Dan listened in his quiet way, then said, "Walk in God's light and pay no attention to what any of the rest of us say."

Sound advice, indeed!

Prayer: Father God, I identify with Aesop's fable of the man trying to please everyone. That's how I feel as people express their opinions to me. I want to tell them to mind their own business, but such a retort would just start an argument instead of solving anything. So may I walk in your light. May I answer challenges calmly and with respect.

Thoughts to Ponder

1. Do friends or relatives give you unsolicited advice? If so, what about? If not, why not?

2. How do you respond when others tell you how to raise your children? Are you happy with your usual response? Why or why not?
3. What's the best parenting advice you've ever received? Who gave it?

Personal Ponderings

Day 41

When the Kids Fight
A Referee's Exhaustion

> How good and pleasant it is when God's people live together in unity! Psalm 133:1

Jay and Holly used to have the most ridiculous arguments. One day, I'd just gotten home from work when they met me at the door.

"Mom, ground Holly," Jay demanded. "She threw stuff at me!"

I turned to Holly. "What did you throw at him?"

"String," she conceded.

I sighed and looked at Jay. "What's the big deal? So she threw string at you."

He never batted an eye. "Mom, it was on a large wooden *spool*."

Yes, we single mothers have enough crises to juggle without having to referee within our own homes. But having children at odds often happens.

I remember all too well the tension Jay and Holly, "the greatest kids in the world," each went through while wishing to have been an only child. And in some moments, if they'd kept it up much longer, I could have accommodated that wish easily!

At times, I was convinced they stayed awake at night, thinking up ways to aggravate each other. That started about the time they both were entering puberty, and it was an exhausting time.

For a while, they were so rude to each other I was tempted not to write about single parenting. One exhausting afternoon I listened to another round of "Did not. Did too."

"My editor should hear this," I said. "How can I give advice when you two argue so?"

Jay barely glanced my way. "Just have a section called 'When the Kids Fight.'"

I frowned. "But we've been through so much together! And we've got enough battles outside; we don't need to face more *inside* these walls! We've got to get through this as friends!"

They looked at each other and laughed. So much for my manipulation by guilt.

Yes, their quarreling was exhausting, but gradually peace came again. I like thinking two simple house rules made the difference:

Rule One: No battles, either physically or verbally.

Rule Two: You don't have to like one another, but you do have to respect each other.

My two young teens didn't always stick to those rules, but just knowing I expected such decent behavior helped keep them on track. I'm convinced youngsters will eventually meet our expectations, so I tried to say encouraging things such as, "You're a neat kid. I'm surprised you said anything that mean."

By the time they hit their late teens, they were friends again. In fact, one afternoon as Holly and I ran errands, she said, "You know, Mom, Jay's really neat. I like talking to him."

I almost wrecked the car as I whipped my head around to see who'd said that.

As my kids got older, they wonderfully moved past the constant bickering. They talked, double-dated, and even ran errands together. Often I stood by the front window, waving good-bye and marveling at the miracle of their friendship.

How did it happen? If I knew *exactly*, I'd go on a packed-house lecture tour.

Oh, I want to take credit and say my involvement with my teens, my demand for mutual respect, our constant communication, and lots of prayer brought us to this refreshing understanding. But, in reality, their eventual maturity had more to do with it than anything else.

> *My two young teens didn't always stick to those rules, but just knowing I expected such decent behavior helped keep them on track.*

I hope the news that my kiddos outgrew arguing is encouraging if your children still are in that stage. But if your children aren't friends yet, let's look at some of the times when they, especially the little ones, are prone to fight. Always, of course, those arguments occur at the most inconvenient or awkward moments for us mothers. Kids can square off anytime at the drop of a hat, but the following situations rank among their favorites for sparring with one another:

Whenever the phone rings: Every mother knows as soon as she reaches for her ringing phone, the kids look at each other and say, "What can we get into? I know; let's fight."

Nancy keeps special games nearby that the children can play with only when she's on the phone. That's solved a big problem.

> *Every mother knows as soon as she reaches for her ringing phone, the kids look at each other and say, "What can we get into? I know; let's fight."*

Just before the evening meal: Often kids fight in the hour before dinner. As soon as Sheila gets home from work, her youngsters help make the dinner salads and eat those right away. Some moms keep sliced carrots and quartered apples handy.

Yes, it takes time to prepare those food items ahead of time, but since most kids prefer eating to arguing, planning ahead keeps them from feuding and lets the moms change out of their work clothes without first having to referee another unscheduled bout.

When Mom is most tired: With my kids, it seemed the biggest arguments started when I was the most tired. To keep from yelling, I would ask them to suggest their own solutions for the current difficulty. Holly's suggestions invariably were reasonable, and Jay's usually were dramatic. But their comments allowed us to breathe and get through the crisis of the moment.

Always in the car: My two youngsters had vastly differing tastes in music, so it seemed as soon as we were in the car, they started arguing over the radio stations. My standard solution was uncreative, but it worked: "If you two can't agree, you'll listen to the station I like."

They quickly learned listening to my music was worse than listening to each other's, so they compromised.

Yes, refereeing frequent arguments is exhausting, but creative solutions and maturity help.

Prayer: *Father God, single parenting is exhausting enough without my having to deal with arguments in my own home. We should be getting along, even having fun. Instead, petty issues cause irritations, which turn into resentments and then create battles. Sigh. Please help me find creative, peaceful solutions to this bickering. I am so tired. Hmm. Is this how you feel when your children argue here on earth?*

Thoughts to Ponder

1. If you have more than one child, do they argue? Why or why not?
2. What situations trigger arguments between your children or extended family?
3. What solutions do you offer as you attempt to referee ongoing issues?

Personal Ponderings

_____

_____

_____

Understanding the Battles

Day 42

Hope Abounds

What causes fights and quarrels among you? Don't they come from your desires that battle within you? James 4:1

Did you have siblings when you were growing up? If so, did all of you always get along? If you were an only child, were you surprised to learn that sisters and brothers occasionally argue? Sadly, arguments are as old as humankind. And while we may nod over ancient communities being at odds, we don't like warfare in our homes. In fact, have you ever said to your children, "Why can't you just get along?"

Yes, we all want peace. So let's look at two reasons often behind our children's battles:

They're dealing with their own stress. When we are trying to pay bills, deal with a mountain of responsibilities, and wade through the grief of death or divorce or broken dreams, it's easy to forget that our children are dealing with their own challenges. Add in the bodily changes that come with puberty and even our once compliant children may have short fuses.

They're trying to establish their own identity. I've found teens are often at odds because they're trying to pull away from the family unit. That's tension enough, but add a sibling or two going through their own crises and we have the potential for a battle.

They're feeling they don't have a voice. We don't like feeling we aren't in control of our life, that we don't have a say in matters that affect us, so why should our children be any different?

You undoubtedly can add your own reasons for why your young-sters argue. Yes, we all want peace. We know our yelling, "Shut up!" merely creates more tension and noise. We've learned making them feel guilty or playing favorites doesn't solve anything either. So let's look at a few ways to win a cease-fire.

Involve them in the solutions. Since the biggest arguments in our home seemed to start when I was the most tired, I gave myself time to catch my breath by asking the kiddos for their suggestions for solutions. "How would you handle this if you were the mom and I was the child?" was my favorite question.

As I shared previously, Holly's solutions were practical. "I'd send us to separate rooms until we can get along."

Jay would be dramatic. "Remind us how difficult it is to raise kids alone. Remind us you didn't run away to Tahiti or to Ken-tucky when Dad died. Tell us again how that ancient relative gave up her children when she remarried. And we'll remind you her youngest boy wouldn't go to his mother's funeral years later."

By the time they'd offered solutions, I was smiling, we were calmer, and the initial tension had lessened.

When Keri asked her ten-year-old son how he'd solve their argument, she was surprised to hear, "I'd ask the kid what happened at school today to make him so grouchy."

> *When Keri asked her ten-year-old son how he'd solve their argument, she was surprised to hear, "I'd ask the kid what happened at school today to make him so grouchy."*

Give each child separate time. Spend-ing some weekend evenings together one-on-one worked for us. So while Holly babysat, Jay and I usually went out for hamburgers and talked. When it was Holly's turn for alone time, she and I chatted over sandwiches at our favorite tea shop.

Just as children need personal space—whether it's as grand as having their own room or as simple as owning a brightly colored "secrets" box—sometimes they need to have their parent to themselves. In fact, if children know they'll have uninterrupted time alone with their parent later, they're less apt to be so demanding beforehand.

> *We try to treat our children equally. But we can't treat them the same because they aren't the same.*

Treat them as individuals. We try to treat our children equally. But we can't treat them the same because they aren't the same. Often when our sons have a problem, they may want to be left alone until they've worked it out mentally. Our daughters, on the other hand, may want to discuss every detail of their thought process.

Sure, it's exhausting trying to treat children as individuals, but so is trying to undo the damage from raising cookie-cutter kids.

Speaking of equality, do your children ever argue about who should get the larger half of the last piece of pizza or dessert? Mine did—until I had one child cut the item in two and then give the other child first choice. Yes, the ruler came into use more than once as the item was measured seemingly to the smallest atom, but no arguments occurred.

Get it in writing. Just as the contract Holly had written about dating earlier got us both over a few rough spots, so have the other contracts the kids and I drew up concerning curfew, grades, and social life. The written words defined our agreements and stopped future arguments. Besides, those contracts helped me remember exactly what I had said.

Achieve an armistice with prayer. Several years ago, it had been another one of those frustrating days when I didn't need to face two warring youngsters. But as soon as I hit the door, they both wanted to tell their side of the story, namely whose turn it was to get the TV. I sighed and said, "You two must hold secret meetings at night to plan how you can drive me nuts!"

I didn't even have my coat off yet, but we sat on the carpeted stairs as I listened to both sides of the argument. Then I muttered, "I gotta pray about this."

Still on the stairs, I started with a simple, "Father, I hate days like this. I identify more with Saul's craziness than Solomon's wisdom, so please show me how to solve this."

Jay and Holly didn't offer to pray then, and I didn't make them. They needed space. I sent them to their rooms, said they couldn't watch TV for the rest of the evening, and added I didn't want to see them until dinner, thirty minutes later. We'd work out a TV schedule then.

At a mothers' luncheon where I spoke sometime later, I shared my honest prayer. Afterward, another mother scolded me for *not* making my children pray aloud right then. She declared she does that all the time and her children never even raise their voices in the house.

She also let me know if I were a truly spiritual mother, my children would have done the right thing immediately. I asked her how old her children are.

"Six and nine," she answered.

"That's wonderful," I said. But what I meant was, "Let's talk again in about five years."

Keep working for peace. Truthfully, I didn't want my children to be little robots. I wanted them to learn to work through problems and see God as their heavenly Father, to whom they can go whether they're happy or hurting.

Maybe, just maybe, by seeing me turn to the Lord for solutions, my kiddos learned he's ready to listen to anything.

> *"Father, I hate days like this. I identify more with Saul's craziness than Solomon's wisdom, so please show me how to solve this."*

Prayer: Father God, I'm grateful you want us to invite you into every detail of our lives. Thank you that nothing surprises you, not even the arguments that grow out of our many disappointments and stresses. Help me as a mother to teach my children to identify the true cause of their arguments and then solve each battle peacefully. And help me respond to their arguments with wisdom instead of pouring my own anger into an already tense situation. Again, this prayer boils down to one word: "Help!" And to that I'll add "Please" and "Thank You."

Thoughts to Ponder

1. What external tensions or internal conditions cause the most arguments within your home?
2. How do you normally stop the arguments? Does your usual solution work? If so, why? If not, what changes would you like to make?
3. If your children are old enough to analyze the arguments, do you involve them in the solutions? If so, have their suggestions worked? If you haven't involved your youngsters, do you think it would work for your family? Why or why not?

Personal Ponderings

An Attitude of Gratitude

Day 43

The Power of Thankfulness

Let the message of Christ dwell among you richly as you teach and admonish one another with all wisdom through psalms, hymns, and songs from the Spirit, singing to God with gratitude in your hearts. Colossians 3:16

Remember the song "Count Your Blessings"? If you do, then you recall the lyrics telling us to concentrate on our blessings instead of life's challenges. But often that's difficult to do, isn't it? Those are the days I try to remind myself about a story my friend Lanson Ross tells about his school years.

Lanson said his mother wasn't the best cook in the world. To prove that point, he told how every morning she made the same thing for breakfast: oatmeal. She'd boil the water, throw in the oats, throw in the salt, but never stir the ingredients! So when Lanson went downstairs to eat, he never knew if his mother would serve the top part that was all raw, the side part that was all salt, or the burned portion from the bottom of the pan. He just knew he was going to get a bowl of *bad* oatmeal.

This was before the days of being able to stop at a fast-food place on the way to school and buy a sausage and egg biscuit sandwich. If you were a growing boy and hungry, you ate what was available.

Lanson shared the bedroom with a younger brother who was one of those cheerful morning guys. You know the type: someone who tap-dances while he buttons his shirt and whistles as he combs his hair. Normally, Lanson ignored him. But one morning Lanson was especially hungry and especially grumpy.

So he turned to his brother and snarled, "How can you be so cheerful every morning? You know we're going downstairs to the *same bad oatmeal*."

His brother stopped whistling and looked at Lanson in surprise. "Oh, no!" he said. "It's never the *same*. We don't know if we're going to get the raw part or the salty part or the burned part. But it's never the same!"

One situation but two different responses.

At one time or another, life hands all of us repeated bowls of *bad* oatmeal. And I'm convinced our attitude will make a big difference in how we handle those situations. In fact, it may even make a difference in the outcome.

Ever notice how a good attitude can brighten not only our day, but that of the people around us? Want to test my theory? Give a quick smile to others in the store or at the post office. Most folks will return your smile. And maybe even will feel better about their day.

> *Ever notice how a good attitude can brighten not only our day, but that of the people around us?*

What's the basic ingredient for a good attitude? Gratitude.

Wrapping a thankful attitude around ourselves allows us to live with joy and provides a way to rejoin life when we momentarily feel estranged from it. More than that, having a thankful spirit helps us laugh and love with genuine abandon. After all, we don't want to wither inwardly and become bitter, mirthless creatures, a drag on ourselves and everyone around us.

Have you seen the bumper sticker that says, "Develop an Attitude of Gratitude"? The sticker has just enough room to tell us what to do, but it doesn't tell us how to do it. So if you need some help in developing this coveted attitude, here's how to start the process:

Pray. Our heavenly Father knows our thoughts, so our honest prayers are no surprise to him. We safely can dump our disappointments, our anguish, and our complaints on him. So talk to him about all the challenges that have pulled the joy out of you. Tell him you don't feel like counting your blessings when you don't feel as though you have any to count. Ask him to help you see what you can be thankful about. I love it that when

What's the basic ingredient for a good attitude? Gratitude.

we pray, he greets us with open arms instead of a stern, "What? Is it you *again?*" Then he invites us to talk to him about everything, including our frustrations and disappointments. Of course, he already knows the details, but often we need to hear ourselves verbalizing our needs as we turn them over to him.

After we've told him our disappointments, thanked him for listening, and then asked for his help, we can take three practical actions:

Every day, offer someone a sincere compliment or thank-you. Often most of us are like that dear old husband who loved his wife *so* much he *almost* told her! So let's comment on the good things our children do before we complain about all the things they don't do. Even acknowledging when they carry their dishes to the kitchen after supper will encourage them. After all, we enjoy being appreciated. So do our children.

And we don't have to limit those compliments to happenings within our own home. We can offer compliments when we see folks doing nice things for others. I remember the teen who stepped away from his friends to help a mother maneuver her baby stroller down some building steps. The mother nodded her thanks and hurried on. But as I passed the teen, I quietly said, "That was nice of you, young man." His smile let me know he appreciated that someone noticed his effort.

Of course, we thank the store clerks who wait on us and the gracious people who hold a door open for us, but what about those folks who were kind to us long ago? Maybe it's time to write a note of gratitude to the sixth-grade teacher who made history lessons fun. What about calling the aunt who secured circus tickets when we were eight? It's never too late to express gratitude—and never too late to brighten another person's day.

Every day, find something new for which you can thank God. This step is fun as we try to find a new object of our gratitude. Have you ever thanked him for the public library? Ever thanked him for your favorite color? Ever thanked him you can smell a rose? Ever thanked him you can smell a *skunk*? I did! Let me tell you about that.

Most of us are like that dear old husband who loved his wife so much he almost told her!

A few years ago I'd been so ill with bronchitis that I lost my sense of smell. This is a bland world when we can't smell coffee brewing, or the fragrance of the flowers arranged outside the shop near our work, or the scent of the fresh air after a gentle rain, or the pungent smell of our favorite spice as we cook. Two years after my illness, I'd gotten used to not being able to smell my favorite things, but I still missed the sweet fragrance of the deep pink blossoms on the lone rosebush in my tiny backyard.

One June morning as I worked at my desk, I looked out the open window at the new blooms just a few feet away. Suddenly a stinging smell came through the open front door. I wrinkled my nose and said, "Ugh. A skunk!" Then the joyous realization hit me, and I shouted, "Oh! A skunk! I can smell a skunk! Thank you!" I hurried into the backyard and plunged my face into the rose blossoms. You see, I knew if I could smell the skunk, I could smell the roses.

Every day, thank God for something for which you are not happy.
Yes, this one is tough, especially when our children are arguing, unpaid bills are lying on the table, work isn't going well, and each new day seems to send another unwelcome surprise our way. But finding even the smallest things for which we can whisper, "Thank you" during tough times will encourage us that maybe, just maybe, we can find other good things. And if we can't thank God *for* a particular event, we can thank him that we do not face our problems alone. Yes, the battle may be the same, but he is our strong weapon to help us face it. Remember, we do not pray to air! So let's thank our heavenly Father as we invite him into each day's challenges.

Prayer: Father God, I confess I've been so busy dealing with each day's struggles that I forget to look for the blessings. So let me start by thanking you for inviting me to talk to you about anything and everything. Thank you for caring about everything that troubles me. Thank you that I can come to you boldly because of the shed blood of your beloved Son, Jesus. Yes, I wish you were open to my suggestions, but you are not a celestial bellboy I order around. You are Creator of the Universe, Maker of Heaven and Earth. May I remember that fact as I ask for your help. And may I concentrate on each day's blessings instead of allowing myself to be pulled down by the challenges.

Thoughts to Ponder

1. What things or people or situations are you the most grateful for? Why? Have you thanked our heavenly Father for them?
2. Have you ever surprised anyone by offering a sincere compliment or thank-you? If so, how did that person react? If you are hesitant, why do you think that is?

3. What situations in life are difficult for you to offer gratitude for? Do you think you ever will see any good coming out of them? Why or why not?

Personal Ponderings

_____

_____

_____

_____

Day 44

Surprising Encouragement

Little Acts, Big Help

I thank my God every time I remember you. Philippians 1:3

Several years ago on a church trip, Jay, Holly, and I shared a bus with a group from Mexico City who were visiting the area. We couldn't communicate with them, but we smiled and nodded at each other as our separate guides explained the various historical sites.

It was a long day, and by the time our bus stopped for dinner, I was exhausted. As we lined up for the washroom, I rested my arms on top of Holly's head, thinking of the day's chaos.

I had been cheated in a souvenir purchase. I had momentarily lost Jay twice. I had tripped over Holly all day since she insisted on being as close to me as possible because of the new and, to her, frightening scenes. Basically, I thought I'd made a mistake in taking the trip. Soon my thoughts escalated into the conviction that single parenting was a mistake too. From there, I concluded *I* was a mistake! Convinced I couldn't handle the insurmountable challenge life had handed me, my weary thought, "Lord, I can't do this!" welled up.

> *Her words were just as though God himself stepped in to say, "Oh, stop. You can do this because I am with you."*

Right at that moment, one of the Mexican grandmothers returning from the washroom stopped beside me, patted my arm, and said in her halting English, "You good mama."

Her words were just as though God himself stepped in to say, "Oh, stop. You *can* do this because I am with you."

Suddenly, I wasn't quite so tired—or defeated.

I wish I could tell you that was the last time I doubted myself. Instead, there were plenty of situations when I yelped to the Lord about the unfairness of life and the tough road I had to walk.

But I am grateful that when I ask our heavenly Father for some encouragement or a pat on the back, he's quick to give it. But not always the way I expect—or want.

For example, I remember one Michigan Saturday that wasn't going well at all. I was having trouble balancing the checkbook, the washing machine was acting up, and my mechanic said the car's rocker arm, whatever that is, had to be replaced.

I wanted to run away but settled for taking the three of us out for hamburgers. As we walked into the restaurant, I saw that one of my former students—I'll call her Donna—was a waitress there. *Oh, goody,* I thought sarcastically, *I'm tired and discouraged and I run into one of the most obnoxious students I had in fifteen years of teaching.* I still could picture her in the front row of fifth-hour classical mythology, arms folded and eyes daring me to make the lesson interesting. But I wasn't going to disappoint Jay and Holly by leaving. I decided I'd just pretend I hadn't seen her. *Lord, keep us out of her section, please,* I prayed inwardly.

And where did the hostess lead us? Right to Donna's section, of course. But just as I started to ask for another booth, Donna spotted us and came rushing over.

"Mrs. Aldrich! This is so neat!"

Sure, it'll be easier to poison me this way, I thought. But I managed a feeble smile.

"Guess what!" she said. "I'm a Christian now!"

I stood there dumbstruck as my mouth dropped open.

> *But I couldn't get what you and my sister said out of my mind. And last year, I got saved! Isn't that neat?"*

Donna just kept bubbling on. "My sister got saved at college," she said. "And it bugged me that she was always witnessing to me. Then I'd go to your class, and you'd compare the Bible to what the Greeks believed, and I'd get angry all over again. But I couldn't get what you and my sister said out of my mind. And last year, I got saved! Isn't that neat?"

I was too choked up to talk, so I just gave her a hug.

Our hamburgers that night tasted wonderful.

Even though Donna was the last person I wanted to meet in my weary state, she turned out to be the exact blessing I needed that day. The experience made me remember other times God used unexpected people to encourage me and, occasionally, even protect my children.

For example, when Jay was a toddler and his sister just three months old, I had to run some errands. Everything had gone well, even with the baby in my left arm, my purse slung over my shoulder, the purchases in my left hand, and twenty-month-old Jay's hand clutched in my right hand.

As we approached the escalator, I let go of Jay for just a second to steady myself. Quickly I reached for him, but he stepped back, unsure of getting on anything that moved. The escalator was taking me away as he stood watching. Before I had a chance to panic, though, an older couple walked up behind Jay.

That's what I continue to trust the Lord for as I pray—that he will supply the right people or the right experiences to grab hold of my children when I can't.

"Please grab his hand," I said. The couple nodded and brought my smiling little boy with them. They were there when I couldn't be.

That's what I continue to trust the Lord for as I pray—that he will supply the right people or the right experiences to grab hold of my children when I can't.

And as I pray, I'm remembering the older couple that "just happened" to appear at the precise moment I needed them. God does care. That's what I hang on to when the doubts creep in.

Prayer: Father God, I do need encouragement often. But I'm quick to tell you how and through whom it should arrive. So help me take a deep breath and then accept and even rejoice in your unexpected blessings. And please help me trust my children to you. I identify with the image of being on an escalator that's moving me away from my innocent children. Please provide the right people to come along at the right time. I can't do this single-parenting thing without you.

Thoughts to Ponder

1. When do you need the most encouragement?
2. Has anyone unexpectedly given you much-needed encouragement? If so, what was the situation? How did you react?
3. Has anyone provided encouragement or protection for your children? If so, when? If not, have those actions ever been needed? What happened?

Personal Ponderings

_____

_____

_____

_____

Day
45

Help Comes
from Many Sources

From the Tough to the Gentle

God is our refuge and strength, an ever-present help in trouble.
Psalm 46:1

When Jay turned thirteen, I was struggling with finding the balance between letting him have fun and forcing him to be, as he put it, "a wimp."

The scene was one of those this-business-of-raising-kids-alone-is-tough episodes. We were at Lake Michigan, and Jay came in all excited about this wonderful new game he, Erik, and Andy had of jumping out of a moving boat.

Horrified, I gave the typical, teary-eyed mother arguments about the danger of what he was doing. But he said he could handle it.

Then I launched into an account of a brilliant former student who had been killed in a freak accident at his college. Next I described one of our distant relatives who had been killed by his own boat motor when he fell into the lake. I pulled out every horror story I'd ever heard.

> *Sometimes we have to do the hard thing for the future good of a youngster, whether it's calling a counselor or the police.*

Still, Jay remained insistent he and his friends would be fine. I was just worrying too much, he told me.

Then in a sudden burst of what I'm convinced was God-directed inspiration, I called the Coast Guard, explained the situation, and asked if I was overreacting. The officer assured me I wasn't and said not only were the boys' activities stupid, but they were a good way to get killed.

I asked if he'd tell Jay what he had just told me.

"Yes, put him on," he answered. "I'm tired of pulling bodies out of the lake."

Jay accepted the phone grudgingly and with a teen's greeting said, "Yeah?"

I heard the officer's sharp retort even though I couldn't hear his words. Immediately Jay sat straighter.

"Uh, I mean, yes, sir!"

For the next several minutes, Jay listened, and occasionally nodded. Finally, he signed off with, "Okay. Thank you—sir."

I never heard details, but as far as I know, the boys didn't play the game again.

That call may very well have saved young teens' lives. Sometimes we have to do the hard thing for the future good of a youngster, whether it's calling a counselor or the police.

Neither of us had the foggiest notion how to tie a four-in-hand, so I asked a neighbor to teach him.

It's ironic—and maddening at times—but kids often will receive counsel from others that they will not accept from their parents. You know how that goes: Good Ol' Mom is nice to have around sometimes, but really, what does she know?

So whatever the need is and whenever it's necessary, don't be afraid to bring in the heavy artillery of trained professionals. In addition to Coast Guard officers, those professionals can come in the form of counselors, youth pastors, social workers, policemen, or teachers. If you need help, make that all-important call.

Often, though, help can come from ordinary neighbors and friends. When we lived in Michigan, ten-year-old Jay had to wear a tie for his school's spring concert. Neither of us had the foggiest notion how to tie a four-in-hand, so I asked a neighbor to teach him. The neighbor did, bless him, and Jay was ready for his concert.

I remember a young mother who was having trouble potty training her two-year-old son. None of her male relatives were close by to show the little guy how to tackle this ability. So she confided in her neighbor and, with some embarrassment, stammered her request for help.

As a result, each evening for the next couple of weeks, she took her son to the neighbor's house so the husband could give the little fellow a lesson. It worked!

Another idea is to drop colored ice cubes into the toilet bowl and encourage the little guy to fire away. Colored cereal pieces work also.

Help and encouragement can come from our children as well. Chloe's fourteen-year-old daughter, Abby, prepared a lovely meatball dinner the night of what would have been her parents' fifteenth wedding anniversary. As her twelve-year-old brother, Zach, held the chair for their astonished mother, Abby gave a little speech:

"Even though you and Dad are divorced, Zach and I are glad you met. After all, you had us! So, thanks!"

When Zella refused to get the abortion her boyfriend demanded, he left the state without a forwarding address. She gave birth to a son and worked two jobs throughout his school years to support them. When he graduated, he held his diploma high and shouted, "Thanks, Mom!"

She cried with joy throughout the rest of the ceremony.

Youngsters also can lighten their mom's load in their own way. A young Jay heard me tell a friend I'd appreciate her prayers as the date of what would have been my twentieth wedding anniversary loomed.

The kiddos' dad had promised for the Big Two-O to ask me to marry him, so I dreaded facing that lonely time. You see, my husband had never asked me to marry him. Years before, when we were in college, he simply *told* me we were getting married at semester break. And we did.

Several years and two children into our marriage, I thought about the missing proposal and told my husband I wanted to be asked.

He looked up from watching a televised sporting event. "Okay. I'll ask you

"Even though you and Dad are divorced, Zach and I are glad you met. After all, you had us! So, thanks!"

for our twentieth anniversary. Maybe we even will go to Scotland."

He turned back to the TV, but I mentally hugged that future event. We'd visit his Bathgate cousins and walk the moors near his grandparents' ancestral home. He'd pluck sprigs of purple heather, which he'd hand to me as he lovingly whispered, "I love you. Will you marry me?" Sigh. Yes, my heart held that scene even though my head knew in reality he'd golf at St. Andrew's while I walked the moor with his cousin Jean. But sadly, neither event happened.

So on the night of what would have been that special twentieth anniversary, I worked at my desk after Jay and Holly had gone to bed. Soon Jay meandered into my office, stammered another "Good night, Mom," and wandered out. Within five minutes, he did that twice more.

Finally, I said, "Jay, what *is* it?"

He shuffled from one foot to the other in that embarrassed way common to young teens.

At last he blurted, "Mom, will you marry my dad?"

Softly, I answered, "You bet I will, Jay."

I finally could say I had been asked.

Prayer: Father God, I know we need help, but it's so hard to ask. You know the issues I'm dealing with as a single mom, and you know what my children face. So I trust you to guide me to the right people. And I ask that you will show me the help and encouragement available through organizations, friends, and even my own children. But first I need to thank you that I've asked for your help. My asking is a major step in the right direction.

Thoughts to Ponder

1. What's your reaction to the conversation with the Coast Guard?
2. Have you ever needed to ask for professional help for your children? If so, what was the situation? If not, are you open to making such a call if necessary?
3. Have your children unexpectedly provided help or encouragement? If so, describe the event. If not, how would you like them to help?

Personal Ponderings

Day 46

Many Opportunities
For Church and Others

So do not fear for I am with you; do not be dismayed, for I am your God. I will strengthen you and help you; I will uphold you with my righteous right hand. Isaiah 41:10

In the early days of my singlehood, friends said, "Call me if you need anything."

But I didn't call anyone for several months. Why? Because I had so many needs I didn't know where to begin.

Then one Saturday morning, a flat tire forced me into the unfamiliar world of car maintenance. My husband and I had settled into traditional roles: I took care of the house, and he took care of the cars. I didn't have a clue where to go for a new set of tires. So I called a longtime friend from church. All he had to do was recommend the tire store he trusted for his vehicle.

Instead he snapped, "Now that you are alone, you're going to have to figure things like this out for yourself."

I was so stunned at his admonishment I stammered, "You're right," and then hung up.

Obviously, I didn't ask for his help again.

Now, these years later, on behalf of all single moms, here's what I wish I had been able to verbalize then to both my church family and my friends.

Pleas for My Church

Please welcome my family: One of America's greatest mission fields may be in church pews every Sunday. What a great opportunity—to have a life-changing influence on a child.

We can't always depend on our own families to provide the encouragement we need, especially if we live across the country from them. So a good church will do wonders in seeing our kids through rough times. Oh, we have no guarantee church involvement will keep them out of trouble, but our chances for survival are much better.

One of America's greatest mission fields may be in church pews every Sunday.

And please remember that accepting a divorced person isn't the same as condoning divorce. At a civic club luncheon a friend—I'll call him Mike—happened to be seated next to the pastor of a large church. Thinking of his newly divorced sister, Mike asked the pastor what programs the church had for divorced, single parents.

The pastor buttered a roll. "We don't believe in divorce."

"I know," Mike said. "Divorce breaks God's heart too. But surely a church as large as yours has members who have suffered that pain but want to grow in their faith and want their children in a godly environment. How do you help them?"

The pastor frowned. "I said we don't believe in divorce."

Mike sighed. "Oh, I get it. If they divorce, they leave your church."

A shrug was Mike's only answer.

Please remember we are still a family. If your church has several departments, please include single-parent families in the family ministries. And don't expect us single moms to return to the never-married singles group. Our challenges and interests no longer fit that lifestyle.

Accepting a divorced person isn't the same as condoning divorce.

Please talk to me. When you see me in church, please offer a sincere greeting. If my children are small, I'm especially hungry for adult conversation. I often feel awkward in church, and your smile and greeting when I come will make a big difference.

When you ask how I am, please hang around for the answer. If you'll take an interest for even a few minutes in what I'm doing, I won't feel so alone.

Please talk to my children. Even a two-minute chat as you ask specific questions about my son's interests will make him look forward to coming to church and will help him feel less invisible.

Please extend common courtesy. Most single mothers can tell about being asked to move to a different table at a banquet because two couples wanted to sit together. Not only is the request rude, but it tells the single woman that her preference doesn't matter.

And please don't talk about the upcoming Valentine's Day gatherings in front of me. I may be reading the bulletin board in the cloakroom, but I'm also hearing you. Am I being overly sensitive? Yes. But in the early days of singlehood those discussions remind me of additional losses and make me feel all the more invisible.

Please offer practical help. Many churches have auto clinic days when single moms can bring in their cars for tune-ups, oil changes, or winterizing. Other churches keep a file of handymen who are available to help with home repairs—and assign the men to work in teams of two. That wisdom protects both the workers and the single mother.

> *When you ask how I am, please hang around for the answer. If you'll take an interest for even a few minutes in what I'm doing, I won't feel so alone.*

Pleas for My Friends

Please be patient with me. In the early days of being single again, I'm frightened. Yes, this is unfamiliar territory. But I'm not asking you to carry me over this stone-filled road. I'm just asking you to let me put my hand on your shoulder while I shake pebbles out of my shoes.

Please pray for me. I may appear strong, but the load of single parenting and career juggling is heavy. As you pray, if the Lord gives you specific direction, please listen. He knows my needs, whether it's for a recommendation for a good mechanic, for help with grocery money, or for someone to take my son to the Father/Son Banquet at church. If my children are young, it would be great if you'd offer to take them shopping for my Christmas present.

Please include my children. The only fun traditional family my children might remember is yours. What a wonderful ministry you can have just by inviting them to join you and your family for a picnic or game night. Please understand I'm not asking you to raise my children. That's my job. But many young boys and girls have no idea what godly fathers do since they either don't remember their dad or never see him make wise decisions.

And don't discount the importance of just a few minutes of attention. When I was twelve years old, the course of my life was changed in a five-minute meeting with my elderly neighbor's niece, Doris Schumacher. Doris taught English and social studies in Minneapolis and, by her example, showed me that education would be my key to a bright future.

Please understand we are not contagious. I don't want to be feared or pitied. I just want to be treated normally. Simply invite us into your home just as you would any other family. And please accept when I invite your family to my home. Just by being a friend, you will be a blessing in my life and in the lives of my children. And perhaps we can be a blessing in yours.

Prayer: Father God, I don't want to ask for help. I'm afraid of rude remarks, ridicule, judgmental attitudes, rejection. But if I don't ask, I might rob my children of needed guidance or provision. So I'll start by trusting you and asking for your help. This single-parenting road is indeed filled with stones. But you are greater than this path, and I am grateful for your presence.

Thoughts to Ponder

1. What decisions do you need help with?
2. Do you have anyone you can call when you are facing unfamiliar decisions? If so, who? If not, why not?
3. What would you like to tell your married friends or your church about single parenting?

Personal Ponderings

Day 47 An Old Woman's Lesson

Joy on a Grumpy Morning

Teach us to number our days, that we may gain a heart of wisdom. Psalm 90:12

This isn't the life I dreamed about. I had planned my husband and I would grow old together, the way my grandparents had. But that didn't happen. Now I have great chunks of memories I can't share with anyone: *What were the names of the couple who lived next door to us in married housing? The ones with the squeaky bed?*

But while I heard the sounds a dying man makes, many of you have heard the sounds a dying marriage or a shattered dream makes. Perhaps even though you are married, you still carry the responsibilities of a single mother because of military deployment, a prison term, job relocation, or an emotionally uninvolved husband. We're back to my earlier comment that no matter how we arrived at our single-parent status, we're all in the same boat.

While we sigh over lost dreams, we need to discard our thoughts that married couples have the perfect life. After all, plenty of folks *are* growing old together and envying those of us who are single. As I shared earlier, as I speak around the country I often quote Isaiah 54:5—"For your Maker is your husband." I've truly lost track of the number of *married* women who have hugged me afterward and whispered, "I wish I had *your* husband." So let's not waste energy on longing for the dreams that haven't come true. Instead let's look for ways to find the joy in each new day.

I gained a good lesson in looking for each day's joy the morning I encountered a woman who appeared to have nothing to offer other than an empty seat in her breakfast booth.

Earlier on that New York Saturday, I had stared into the mirror. The wing of gray hair at my right temple had widened almost overnight. I slowly lowered my hairbrush onto the bathroom counter. It was definitely a day for breakfast at our favorite café.

The coffee shop in the middle of Mount Kisco, New York, was one of those narrow establishments too busy serving food to bother with the latest tile colors or fancy soda machines. The five booths and dozen counter stools had witnessed almost forty years of World Series arguments, weather complaints, and social changes. Through it all the grill sizzled with over-easy eggs and plump hamburgers.

The counter stools were always occupied first, so we three usually had no trouble getting a booth. That morning, however, even the booths were filled. We stood by the door for a moment, surrounded by the combined smells of bacon grease, grilled bagels, and strong coffee, wondering if anyone was about to leave.

Suddenly, an elderly woman in the back booth waved for us to join her. After our move from Michigan, we'd quickly learned New Yorkers are used to sharing their space, so it wasn't an unusual invitation.

> *Suddenly, an elderly woman in the back booth waved for us to join her. After our move from Michigan, we'd quickly learned New Yorkers are used to sharing their space, so it wasn't an unusual invitation.*

We smiled our thanks and walked toward the woman. Holly slid into the booth next to her, while Jay and I sat across from them. I thanked the woman for her kindness, then introduced myself and both teens.

She nodded, but pointed to her ear and shook her head. *Oh dear, she's deaf,* I thought.

We three sat uncomfortably silent, while our hostess continued with her breakfast. Her red, arthritic hands cut the poached egg on toast as I stared at my own hands, knowing someday they would look like hers.

Wasn't it enough I'd found the wider streak of gray hair just that morning? Did I need this second reminder of my mortality too?

As I looked at Jay and Holly and flashed my standard "It's okay" smile, her hands still moved in my side vision. I forced my thoughts to other details of her person. The collar of her flowered navy blue dress peeked over the top of her tightly buttoned maroon sweater. Tinted glasses sat on the end of her nose.

Her hair was silver and covered by a bright blue winter cap. What color had her hair been? Nondescript brunette like mine? Or chestnut, its red highlights reflecting sunlight as her admiring beau watched?

> *Wasn't it enough I'd found the wider streak of gray hair just that morning? Did I need this second reminder of my mortality too?*

Had her swollen hands once gently held babies who grew up and left for exotic places, remembering her only at Christmas and Mother's Day, if then? Had those same hands tenderly sponged the feverish forehead of an ill husband who, despite her care, died, leaving her to grow old alone?

She put her knife and fork across the plate, drank the last of her mug's heavily creamed coffee, then leaned toward Holly. "Why do you go to bed at night?" she asked.

Because we mistakenly had assumed she was mute as well as deaf, her question momentarily startled us. Finally Holly shrugged and answered, "Because I'm tired?"

The woman smiled, the sparkle in her eyes suddenly apparent. "Because the bed won't come to you!"

We three laughed appreciatively then, and she tapped the table surface in front of Jay. "If I put a quarter and a five-cent piece here, and the five-cent piece rolled off, why didn't the quarter roll off too?"

Jay and I looked at each other, puzzled. The woman smiled again as she supplied the answer with obvious delight. "Because the quarter has more sense!"

Her unexpected play on words was so comical, we all laughed. I waited for another riddle, but she busied herself gathering her newspaper and purse. Holly stood to let her out of the booth.

She smiled at me, patted Holly's shoulder, gripped Jay's hand in farewell, and was off, her head up and her stooped shoulders straightened—momentarily, at least—against the day.

> *Had her swollen hands once gently held babies who grew up and left for exotic places, remembering her only at Christmas and Mother's Day, if then?*

The booth suddenly seemed empty. My immediate sense of loss was so evident, Holly asked, "What's wrong, Mom?"

I stared at her. Actually, nothing was wrong, but something was indeed gone. Yes, that was it—her joy. That dear, elderly woman had given us a moment of unexpected joy, a brief time of serendipity, and I wanted to relish it, at least for a little longer.

In those few moments we'd spent with her, I'd seen no self-pity, no laments for what she might have lost, and no admonishment that I enjoy these "best days of life" with my children. She had merely invited us to share her private joy. And, in doing so, she had shown us a more noble way to face challenges.

I smiled at the memory of her sparkling eyes. And the memory helped me accept the new gray streak in my hair as merely another well-earned milestone. *When I'm her age,* I told myself, *I hope I'm also teaching others to grab today's joy.*

For now, though, I'll rejoice in what I have left instead of lamenting what I've lost.

That's not a bad lesson to have learned on a grumpy morning.

Prayer: Father God, I do lament over what used to be. I do grieve lost dreams. But longing for former days or looking at life's many disappointments won't help me deal with today's challenges. Only you can untangle the heartaches. So please help me give each "if only" to you. Please help me be aware of each day's new joy. Thank you for caring about everything that touches me—and my children.

Thoughts to Ponder

1. Do you ever envy married couples? If so, for what reasons? If not, why?
2. Have you ever had a grumpy day joyfully interrupted? If so, what was the situation? If not, when have you needed such an interruption?
3. Do you ever attempt to pass along cheerful wisdom to others? If so, in what ways? If not, what makes you hesitate?

Personal Ponderings

Accepting the Empty Nest

Two Pairs of Apron Strings

Praise be to God, who has not rejected my prayer or withheld his love from me! Psalm 66:20

Most of you aren't approaching the empty nest just yet. I assume you are juggling work and school schedules. Maybe you are still concerned about good child care.

But some of you are watching your teen's excitement about graduating from high school and getting ready for what he or she thinks will be the joyous freedom of college or the work environment. Maybe the thought of an empty house frightens you. But let me assure you that if we've done our job right, our children won't want to stay at home with us forever. Oh, they'll enjoy coming home at holidays, maybe, but for the most part, they'll go their own way. That's supposed to be the end result of our solid parenting—to help make them so strong they will be able to take care of themselves. So don't give in to fear. This new stage of life can be your time to find out who you are beyond the role of single mother.

Yes, it can be scary to restructure our lives when our children move out. After all, they are the ones who have absorbed our time and thoughts and energy and prayer life for so long. So we have to start thinking about that empty nest chapter in our lives long before it happens.

I've always enjoyed taking road trips. When Jay and Holly were little, they went wherever I took them. By their early teens, they still went but complained a lot. In their mid-teens, I could get them to go without complaint only if I let each take a friend along.

Soon we were to the point where they were involved in church youth activities or school events with their friends, so if I wanted to go to a concert or play, I went with *my* friends.

Yes, it was an adjustment, but I didn't want to be so dependent on my children that I couldn't function once they left the nest. Nor did I want to whine to them, "Why don't you call me more often?" Even before they moved out, I knew they wouldn't call me as much as I'd wish. But my goal was for my two children to turn into mature, responsible adults, which would allow me to know I had done my job well. And, yes, all too soon I was wrapping prayers around them as they set off toward their own adventures without me. By then, though, I was comfortable with our separate activities because we had arrived at the new stage in little steps.

> *All too soon I was wrapping prayers around them as they set off toward their own adventures without me.*

But as part of my accepting the empty nest, I had planned a personal little ceremony years before. When Jay graduated from high school, he, Holly, and I celebrated at our favorite restaurant for dinner.

One present from me was a narrow box containing two strips of blue flowered material. As Jay folded back the tissue, he stared at the vaguely familiar pattern for a moment.

Finally, I said, "That's my most important present of all, honey. Those are my apron strings to symbolize you no longer are tied to them."

Jay grinned, and Holly exclaimed, "Wow! Next year do I get apron strings too?"

Groan. The years were passing far too quickly. But sure enough, just a few days later (it seemed) there we were again at our same favorite restaurant. This time it was Holly who was opening presents for *her* high school graduation. When she got to the narrow box, she quickly tore the paper off. Inside, indeed, were the strings from my second apron. Attached was this note:

Dear Holly,
As Jay can tell you, I'll often try to take this gift back. But here are my apron strings to say I really am trying to let you go. Go forward with God. Much love, Mom

Both of those evenings were milestones in our finding new ways to relate—no longer just as parent and child, but as adult to adult. In the process of building a new relationship with my children, I've discovered that new ways of relating are gifts in themselves. And, in case you're wondering, aprons aren't as old-fashioned as some folks might think. Even though I don't cook the way I used to, those aprons covered my work clothes when I got in late and had to throw together a spaghetti dinner. They also went around little waists when it was time to make salt and baking soda school projects. So for me, the cut apron strings symbolized my letting go.

> *Both of those evenings were milestones in our finding new ways to relate— no longer just as parent and child, but as adult to adult.*

What will work for you when that time comes for your family?

Since the presentation of those gifts, I've often thought about the celestial apron strings of freedom our heavenly Father has given us. Freedom to choose our daily routine, freedom to invite him into our decisions (or not), even freedom to disregard his loving guidelines. At times I wish he never had cut those strings for me, since I haven't always chosen the right way. But his gift should encourage us too since it says we are not powerless. We *can* choose the right way, including inviting him into the daily challenges of single parenting. And that's a great gift, indeed.

In preparation for letting go, I began early to adjust to a schedule that includes activities I like. I actually made a list of the local museums and tourist attractions Jay and Holly hadn't been interested in. But I also knew such touristy activity would get old fast, so I pondered ways to expand my speaking and writing. (We Kentucky women have to be kept busy to keep us out of trouble.) And I planned deeper involvement in missions. I didn't want to drive the *adult* Jay and Holly nuts. Even though I had concentrated on them for so many years, I'd seen in the lives of my friends the damage clutchy mothers could do. Thus, I've continued to think of ways to keep my children as my friends long after they stopped being my responsibility.

> *We* can *choose the right way, including inviting him into the daily challenges of single parenting.*

That's my journey, but most single mothers aren't to this place yet. They're still trying to find lost mittens, dropping off little ones at the sitter's or juggling early teen schedules, worrying about unsupervised activities, and trying to plan quality time. If you're one of those moms, allow me to say, "Honey, hang in there! It does get better."

What you're going through now is absolutely exhausting, but your turn *is* coming when you can breathe at a normal rate again.

Even as I wrote the previous paragraph, however, I thought of the old saying, "Just when a mother thinks her work is finished, she becomes a grandmother."

So we are mothers for the long haul, but we have the challenge and joy of watching our loving influence make a difference in another's life. That's heady stuff.

And it makes me smile.

Prayer: Father God, you know my heart. You know my thoughts, my fears, my hopes, my disappointments. And you also know how I'm trying to trust you with the details of my life and those of my children. So I entrust this empty nest issue to you, knowing that what surprises me is never a surprise to you. Thank you for being with me and with my children today and in the days ahead.

Thoughts to Ponder

1. What are your thoughts about the empty nest—either for yourself or what you have witnessed through others?
2. How close are you to the empty nest? What do you dread about this stage of life? What part do you look forward to?
3. Do you have special gifts planned for your children to symbolize their entry into adulthood? If so, what are they? If not yet, what items do you think best fit each child's personality?

Personal Ponderings

<table>
<tr><td>Day
49</td><td># Ignoring the Crowd
Embracing God-Given Strength</td></tr>
</table>

The LORD is near to all who call on him, to all who call on him in truth. Psalm 145:18

A few weeks ago, I watched the classic movie *The Grapes of Wrath*. Perhaps because it was produced during the Great Depression, when folks were desperate for hope, it ended on a happier note than the book did. I was struck by the film mother's incredible strength as she held her family together. I especially liked her refusal to give up. When the sky is caving in, someone must stand with arms thrust upward, saying, "Come stand by me. It's going to be okay."

That's the type of woman I want to be.

One thing that can keep us from such strength, though, is listening to the wrong voices.

Whenever I run into anyone predicting failure for my latest venture, I try to remember the story my friend Kim told about her son, Trey, who was pitching in a championship Little League game. The tying run was on third base, the winning run on second. On the mound, Trey leaned toward home plate, trying to concentrate on the catcher's signals for this last pitch of the game.

Suddenly, the fans for the opposing team began to jeer, calling, "Loser! You'll never get it over the plate!"

Kim clutched her hands together and whispered, "Come on, Trey. Don't listen to those voices. Remember what we talked about this morning."

On their way to the park just a few hours earlier, Kim had sensed her son's unusual anxiety and asked what was wrong.

"I hate it when the other team's fans yell at me," he answered.

"Do they come onto the field and yell in your face?" she asked, feigning naiveté.

"Well, no," he conceded. "But they make me feel bad, and I can't concentrate."

"Don't listen to the voices," his mom said. "Look at your catcher. Think about the next pitch. Listening to those voices can't take away your ability. But they *can* cause you to defeat yourself."

Now, on the mound, Trey stared at the batter, went into his windup—and delivered strike three to win the game. The voices had no power once he refused to listen to them

We single mothers have numerous times when we feel as Trey did. Yes, we wish the people around us would be quiet. The voices telling us we don't measure up may come at us from people around us now or they may come from the past in memories—comments from a drunken parent, cruel classmate, thoughtless teacher, unstable coworker. But those voices have power only if we listen to them.

I know about those critical voices on the mental disks I'm prone to replay. But I finally have learned to replace those negative messages with these new, strengthening ones:

God didn't bring me this far to leave me alone.

I *can* do this.

This too shall pass.

> *The voices telling us we don't measure up may come at us from people around us now or they may come from the past in memories.*

And my feisty favorite: Keep hanging on to the Lord and don't let the "turkeys" win!

Amazingly, though, just as we get the encouraging mental disks firmly in place and are ready to face the latest challenge, somebody new may come along to announce we don't measure up. Sometimes that person is a stranger.

For example, recently I had my PR photo taken by a local studio. Since the prints were a simple head-and-shoulders shot, I expected them back within a day or two. But when I called, the photographer said I couldn't have them for another week; she'd sent them to the finishing department to have the lines around my eyes airbrushed out.

God didn't bring me this far to leave me alone.

"I don't want those lines airbrushed out," I said. "I've worked hard for them."

"But they make you look middle-aged," she said.

"I *am* middle-aged," I declared. "Leave my wrinkles alone."

I refused to give in, and the photos were ready for pickup that afternoon. And, clearly, the wrinkles of years past were all there, untouched and undiminished by cosmetic artifice.

Yes, every feature, every contour, every experience line was intact, each one a joyous witness to the years the Lord and I have walked in fellowship together, each one a precious reminder of life's tears and joys, each one a powerful testimony to the love and devotion invested in my wonderful children.

Oh, as I look in the mirror, I certainly see the changes of time that come to us all. But I also see a woman who, in her remaining decades, has the privilege of encouraging and teaching younger women.

Do I miss the smooth, firm skin of my youth? Of course. But do I *grieve* its loss? No. Each line represents another milestone in my journey toward becoming the woman God wants me to be. So these same lines are also harbingers of promise to the exciting adventures and fulfilling experiences awaiting me in the years ahead.

Prayer: Father God, I confess I do listen to the critical voices, both from others and even myself. Help me replace the noise of those defeating voices with your gentle promises to be with me. Help me be the woman you have created me to be. Help me rejoice in this day and in who I am because of what you have brought me through. Thank you!

Thoughts to Ponder

1. Do the people around you summarize your failures or dash your dreams? If so, how? If not, have you counted those people who do not among your blessings?
2. What encouragement have you received from others? What encouragement do you offer yourself?
3. List several of your positive qualities or abilities.

Personal Ponderings

Many Faces of Courage

Day 50

Warriors, Workers, and Those Who Pray

> Have I not commanded you? Be strong and courageous. Do not be afraid; do not be discouraged, for the LORD your God will be with you wherever you go. Joshua 1:9

D o you have days when you feel overwhelmed? Maybe even days when you think you don't have an ounce of strength left? Days when you resent it when folks comment on your courage? Days when courageous is the last thing you feel? Days when fear looms, wiping away any hint of personal confidence? Yep, we all have been there.

A while back, I heard a minister say, "Courage is fear that already has said its prayers." I like that. When we're afraid, we exaggerate our fears and say, "I'll never be able to . . ." Most of us have allowed our fears to finish that sentence at one time or another.

Do you recall the dramatic account in the book of Numbers, chapters 13 and 14, when the Israelites heard reports about the Promised Land? The twelve spies Moses had sent there now argued whether they could claim the land.

Two of the warriors, Caleb and Joshua, said, "We *can* do it!"

But the ten others gave in to their fears and told Moses, the people, and themselves they couldn't possibly possess the land because of the size and strength of the groups already living there. In fact, they said, "We seemed like grasshoppers in our own eyes, and we looked the same to them" (Num. 13:33).

That's the way we feel when we're facing a challenge—small and powerless. We allow our fear to make the situation bigger than it really is. And we rob ourselves of a blessing, just as the ten spies who talked the people out of conquering the land did. That fear-filled decision resulted in the Israelites having to endure another forty years of wandering in the desert. I don't know about you, but I don't have another forty years to waste that way.

At one time or another, like the spies in Numbers 13, we all have challenges we're afraid to tackle. What wonderful things would we experience if we claimed God's promises and started looking at life courageously instead of through the eyes of defeat? And it isn't just ancient (or modern) warriors who display courage.

For example, when we lived in New York, we ventured down to the city to watch the Macy's Thanksgiving Day parade with friends—and thousands of others. It was an incredible day of seeing the displays that long had been part of our holiday traditions but only on TV. The best part of the day for me, though, was meeting a subway elevator operator.

For long hours each day he's trapped in a box under the streets of New York City and breathing air thick with dirt and fumes. I wouldn't have blamed him if he'd been grumpy and complained about being stuck there. But he greeted us cheerfully and asked where we were from.

What wonderful things would we experience if we claimed God's promises and started looking at life courageously instead of through the eyes of defeat?

When he had delivered us to our requested level, he wished us well, asked us to come back again, and added a cheerful, "I luv ya."

As we waited for the subway train, we could hear him singing as he strolled in front of the eleva-tor, waiting for his next passengers.

Rather than allowing himself to complain about his life, he chose to bring freshness and joy to those who shared his day, even for those few minutes.

True, the elevator operator wasn't facing the same enemies the Israelites were. But whatever his own struggles, he appeared to face them with cheerful courage and without paralyzing regrets.

Yes, just as fear and bitterness can drain our courage and keep us from a bright future, so can regrets. Years ago, I told a family friend about my regret I'd sold some furniture for too low a price.

> *Hanging on to past regrets doesn't allow us to move forward.*

His gentle advice has since gotten me through more than mere furniture sales: "You've made your decision. Now live with it."

So even as we pray, we need to make a conscious effort to stop the "if onlys," such as "If only I hadn't moved," or "If only I hadn't taken that job," or "If only I hadn't married so young."

Remember, you made your decision based on the information you had at the time. Allow me to say this again: Hanging on to past regrets doesn't allow us to move forward.

A couple of summers ago, a friend was back in her hometown visiting relatives. While her children enjoyed a special outing with their cousins, she drove by the house where she had lived before her divorce. She felt almost as though she should pull into the driveway and honk the horn for her husband to come out and help with the groceries.

But, of course, that was impossible, and she drove away through tears as she scolded herself. *Why didn't I have the good sense to enjoy those years instead of always looking for perfection?* she wondered. *Why was I demanding storybook attention?*

Relief came only as she prayed, asking the Lord's forgiveness for not having appreciated the blessings of ordinary events. Then she asked him to help her see the joy in each new day. In that moment, she let go of the past and was willing to move forward.

During today's devotion, we've looked at regrets and fear of the unknown. But what if the fear is real? Several years ago, Chet Bitterman Jr., a Wycliffe missionary in Bogota, Columbia, was kidnapped. For days, his father furiously paced his Pennsylvania home, wondering how he could rescue his son. Suddenly he heard within his spirit, "Give thanks."

To give thanks was the last thing Chet Sr. wanted to do. He'd already seriously contemplated rounding up an armed group of his friends, flying into the South American city, and taking it apart, brick by brick.

But as he struggled with the Spirit's witness in his heart, he realized the order was to *give* thanks, not *feel* thanks. As he wondered what he could possibly be thankful for, he remembered his son had memorized hundreds of Scripture verses.

Surely those verses are encouraging him, he thought as he gave thanks for the peace the Word of God undoubtedly was giving Chet Jr. at that very moment.

Upon further reflection, Chet Sr. added thankfulness for his son's physical strength and emotional stability. The list grew. Did it provide the miracle the senior Bitterman wanted? Sadly, no. Young Chet's body was found in an abandoned bus forty-eight days later. But the prayers of a worried parent were another act of courage—and opened a hurting heart to the comfort the Lord wanted to give.

But as he struggled with the Spirit's witness in his heart, he realized the order was to give thanks, not feel thanks.

I don't know why our heavenly Father didn't rescue the young missionary who was serving him. And I don't know why he allows bad things to happen to us. All I know is that he is with us always—during good times and bad. So let's be grateful when things are going well and cling to him when the bad times come.

Prayer: *Father God, I don't feel courageous. In fact, fear often seems to be my companion these days. Fear of the future. Fear for my children. Fear about our finances. And now, after reading today's devotion, I have fear of fear! Mixed with those fears are so many regrets. Sigh. But constantly worrying about my fears and failures won't make them go away. So please help me talk to you honestly about each one. Help me recognize your comfort, your forgiveness, your guidance. Help me know you are with me and with my children.*

Thoughts to Ponder

1. What's your definition of courage?
2. Have you ever allowed fear to keep you from a blessing? If so, what was the situation? If not, have you seen fear hold others back?
3. As a single mother, you have performed numerous courageous acts, sometimes even without realizing it at the time. List several and then offer gratitude to the Lord for his help during those times.

Personal Ponderings

Forward in Faith

Better Than Lemonade

Day 51

I call to you, LORD, come quickly to me; hear me when I call to you. Psalm 141:1

We've all heard the saying, "When life hands you lemons, make lemonade!" One of my favorite stories illustrating that thought is from A. Philip Parham's *Letting God: Christian Meditations for Recovering Persons*. Here's how I remember an account he told:

> A church's new minister always left written instructions for his staff. A janitor who could not read or write was fired when he failed to respond to the messages.
>
> But instead of giving in to discouragement, the man began his own cleaning business and eventually became very wealthy.
>
> One day, his banker was astounded when he discovered his customer's illiteracy. "Just imagine where you'd be if you could read and write!" he exclaimed.
>
> The man smiled. "I'd be a janitor at the corner church."

I like that story! Yes, I assume the janitor had a moment, at least, of panic when he was fired. But no matter his initial reaction to losing his job, he ultimately made the bold decision to create something better instead of giving in to despair.

We can do the same as well. When we're facing major decisions, we need to remember the biblical three-step process: pray, read the Word, and seek godly counsel. Do perfect solutions appear immediately? Usually not. In fact, sometimes we can take those important steps and still not have a clear answer as soon as we'd like.

When that happens to me, I know I'm undoubtedly fighting fear. In those paralyzing moments, I ask myself, "A year from now, what am I going to wish I had done?"

I've asked myself that twice—when we moved from Michigan to New York so I could join the editorial staff at a Christian magazine and again when we moved to Colorado when I was offered a senior editorship at another major Christian magazine. Both times, I've answered my worry with, "A year from now I'm going to wish I'd had the courage to go." And both times, I've been glad I took a deep breath and grabbed the adventure.

> *In those paralyzing moments, I ask myself, "A year from now, what am I going to wish I had done?"*

Please hear me: I'm not advocating reckless abandonment of common sense or discarding morality to follow a sinful path. I'm just asking that we not be bound by fear.

I remember when we were facing the move to Colorado. I was convinced the Lord was offering me an incredible job opportunity, and Jay wanted out of New York. There was only one problem: Holly's fears. How could I convince my daughter she *would* survive?

Of course, I was praying constantly—and fretting. Then one evening while Jay and Holly attended a youth activity, Doug and Lou, friends from church, invited me over for dinner. We chatted about parenting and our jobs, and Doug talked about his work with the disabled. One story he told offered the encouragement I needed.

As part of his training, Doug had worked in a hospital. A man had been there for several weeks recovering from an accident, but still was having trouble walking.

The doctors insisted this patient had no physical reason for the tiny, cautious steps he insisted upon, but he ignored their pronouncements that he could walk normally.

Then they assigned Doug to him.

The first afternoon with the man, Doug watched him take those fear-filled steps and asked why he walked like that.

"I'm afraid I'll fall," the man said.

I probably would have told the man, "You won't fall," but Doug merely asked another question:

"Did you ever fall when you were a kid?"

"Sure, lots of times," the man said.

"Where?"

"On the grass."

Doug nodded and asked, "How about when you were older? Did you ever fall then?"

The man smiled. "Sure. I played softball. I was always falling as I dove after a ball or slid into base."

I was convinced the Lord was offering me an incredible job opportunity, and Jay wanted out of New York. There was only one problem: Holly's fears.

Doug nodded again. "Okay, we're going for a walk, and I'm going to trip you. You're going to fall. Then you're going to see it's all right."

The man wasn't sure he could do that, but Doug coaxed him outside to the hospital lawn. As they walked along, talking about their favorite sports teams, Doug suddenly tripped him, just as he had promised he would, and the man sprawled in the grass.

For a moment, he lay still, as though he mentally was checking for broken bones. Everything was okay. He stood up and grinned at Doug. Then he bounced up and down and even gave a little jump. He was going to be just fine.

That evening when I picked up the kiddos from youth group, I put my arm around Holly and retold the story.

Then I gave her an extra squeeze. "So, honey, I'm going to trip you," I said. "But you're going to see God is leading us, and it's going to be okay."

She gave one of her exasperated huffs, but she knew there would be no turning back. Yes, she "plowed ground" with her fingers as she grumpily tried to hang on to the familiar during our drive west. But it didn't take her long to settle in, make new friends, and decide she really liked it here in Colorado. In fact, she's stated she never wants to live anywhere else.

> "*What happens isn't as important as how you react to it.*"

Whew! Yes, a good result came from a tough decision. But we see that truth in the Bible, don't we? After all, most of the psalms we find so uplifting were written during times of difficulty. And several of the epistles with their messages of joy and love were written by Paul while he was in prison chains. How's that for holy encouragement and strength?

My former teaching buddy, Carl, kept this quotation on his classroom board: "What happens isn't as important as how you react to it."

Yes, our attitude will make the difference in whether we're open to the good things God wants to give us. But often we get just what we expect out of life.

Years ago, I invited a perfectly healthy aunt to have dinner with us the following week.

Her reply was immediate: "Oh, I never plan anything. I might be sick."

She missed numerous fun opportunities and even blessings because she was afraid of taking even a tiny risk.

So let's be prayed up and ready to accept the blessings our heavenly Father offers. Good days are ahead!

Prayer: Father God, I don't like change. I like knowing what's around the next corner. But even as I say that, I remember the many times change has been thrust upon me. I had no control over what happened then, but I realize I'm trying to have control over my circumstances now. So help me give the past to you as I work on the things I can do today. And may I be ready to accept the bright future you want to give.

Thoughts to Ponder

1. What dreams have you lost? What steps can you take to regain at least part of them?
2. What does it mean to you to be "prayed up and ready"?
3. Have you ever been "tripped" in life only to discover the good that came as a result?

Personal Ponderings

_____

_____

_____

Embracing the Future

Day 52

Head Up, Shoulders Straightened

For I know the plans I have for you, declares the LORD, plans to prosper you and not to harm you, plans to give you hope and a future. Jeremiah 29:11

With the Lord's help, and as we ask him to bring his good out of our pain, we can do more than merely survive our situation; we can be victorious over it. But we also can't get arrogant about our ability to face the challenges ahead—as I learned during my Michigan days.

John and Elizabeth Sherrill had invited me to Chappaqua, New York, to talk about a writing project. I was elated. And nervous as could be.

New York was the end of the world to me then. How could I fly to LaGuardia Airport, rent a car, and drive the hour north on those mysterious Eastern parkways? But John sent me a map as though he was confident of my ability to handle such a huge challenge.

The plane landed safely, and I picked up the rental car. I studied the map, confident that if I followed it correctly, it would lead me through the area around LaGuardia until I could pick up the route to head north.

I prayed, "Lord, you know I have the worst sense of direction in the world. But I trust you to guide me and get me there safely and back to the airport on time."

With a giant sigh, I put the car into gear and started out through the gate. At each stoplight, I reexamined the map.

Which way, Lord? was my constant question. Amazingly, at every turn I knew the way to go. At one point, the street sign had been knocked down. I cocked my head to decipher the way it had been pointing, but it was as though he was sitting right at my elbow, saying, "Turn left at the next stop."

It was an amazing day. Not only did I spend the day with the Sherrills, but I drove through New York City. Both were miracles for this Harlan County, Kentucky, gal.

My plane back to the Detroit Metro Airport landed on time. I was twenty minutes from home and would drive a route I'd driven dozens of times. As I located my car in the parking lot, I didn't *say* it, but my attitude was one of, "Thanks, God. Now I'll take it from here!" Oops.

An hour later, with my frustration growing, I was still trying to get past new construction and off Ecorse Road. It wasn't until I yelped a prayer for help that I finally got onto I-94 and headed home.

Since then I've often prayed, "Don't let me take it from here again. *Your* will only."

> *I didn't* say *it, but my attitude was one of, "Thanks, God. Now I'll take it from here!" Oops.*

Yes, I learned that night I often can't handle even the most familiar things, so I have to trust the unfamiliar to him always. But I've also learned he wants to help us get back on the right road, if we'll let him.

Because I am God's child, he is concerned about every aspect of my life. I like the three verbs in Luke 11:9: "*Ask* and it will be given to you; *seek* and you will find; *knock* and the door will be opened to you."

Ask, seek, and *knock* are words of action for us. Even as much as we long to be rescued from problems, we still are responsible for the results. The Lord has promised to help us, to direct us, but we still have to work through the challenges and take that first step in faith. I'm grateful he wants us to ask him to help us face our scary responsibilities. Amazingly, as we invite him into our daily challenges, we often receive the needed help in unexpected ways.

I remember we three had been in Colorado only a few weeks when I dropped Jay off at his high school at 4:00 a.m. to catch the bus for a regional event. I had much on my mind, including the roof damage from the latest hail storm, the occasional short circuit in the car's engine, and the state-protected woodpeckers determined to move into our attic. Well, you get the picture.

That morning, instead of going home, I drove to a nearby park noted for the majestic red rock formations. I needed to connect with God, and I thought I could do that best in his world instead of in mine.

As I entered the blackness of the park, I pulled off the narrow road and got out to study the heavens, hoping the beauty of the star-filled sky would offer some encouragement. Suddenly, a bright green meteor shot across the full length of the sky.

Stunned, I said aloud, "Oh! Thank you!" as I watched the trail.

As the vivid, otherworldly color faded into the horizon, my challenges didn't seem as heavy as before. Oh, they were far from being solved, and I still had to deal with the new problems on top of the ones I already was carrying. But I knew the scene would remain with me in the days ahead.

> Ask, seek, *and* knock *are words of action for us.*

I also knew I would not have seen the Creator's glory without the darkness. That's how it is with the challenges we face as single parents. We have the opportunity to be more in tune with his help and his presence because of our situation. Often, all we have to do is look *up*. Remember, Daniel of the Old Testament was not saved *from* the lion's den. He was saved *in* it.

I started this book with the assurance both my children turned out to be wonderful adults despite having been raised in a single-parent household. But even after we had survived major moves, financial crises, and life's various challenges, we still had a surprise or two waiting. Especially when Holly got engaged.

As she and I were making her wedding plans, I realized she was increasingly melancholy. Then, one evening, she lamented that her dad wasn't there to walk her down the aisle. We both cried a little, but she wiped her eyes and decided to ask Jay to escort her. I started praying right then that his normal public reticence wouldn't keep him from assenting to her wish.

The next evening, the three of us gathered in the living room, and Holly made her request. In anticipation of this moment, Jay had prepared a little speech. He managed to get only as far as, "Holly, that's Dad's job" before she, in typical Aldrich family style, stopped him from finishing his sentence.

> *Daniel of the Old Testament was not saved from the lion's den. He was saved in it.*

"But Dad's dead!" she wailed. Jay sighed. "What I was going to say is that's Dad's role, but *Mom* has been the one who has held this family together. *She* should walk you down the aisle."

Now it was my turn to wail. "But Jay, I want to be the mother of the bride," I protested, ignoring the enormous compliment he had given me. "I want to stand up and turn to watch Holly come down the aisle."

Poor Jay. Now he had two crying women to calm down. While he patted first one, then the other on the shoulder, Holly and I blew our noses. Then we all settled down to discuss possible solutions. After my usual open-eyed prayer of "Lord, please help," we finally decided we would "tag team" the event: Jay would walk Holly down the aisle to my pew; then I would step out and give the declaration in answer to the pastor's question, "Who escorts this woman to this man?" (Notice we don't give away women in *this* family.)

No, the solution wasn't our first choice—that one had included her dad—but it was a good one. In fact, as it turned out, the three of us standing together before the altar provided a touching, visible symbol of the team we had been. And all because we invited the Lord into the problem, analyzed our choices, and adjusted to the solution. Not a bad combination in any single-parenting situation.

Now, I realize many of you wish you could apply this solution to your daughter's or son's future marriage. Instead, you will face the challenge of your ex-husband's new wife and family. But I know you can handle the situation with grace and perhaps even humor. After all, I've seen several of my friends do exactly that. For the sake of family peace, and sincere smiles for the wedding photos, they set aside painful memories and bit back sharp comments. And know what? They tell me they slept better after the ceremony because of their decision to enjoy the day. Good for them.

So face the coming challenges with your head high and your shoulders back, dear single mother.

You do have great strength and a bright future as you go forward with God.

Now, as we say good-bye, I'm sending you a heart hug across the miles.

Prayer: Father God, do I really have a bright future? You know the many times I've fallen on my face when my attitude has been one of "I'll take it from here." But you also know the many times I've cried out for your help and have felt your rescue even though I still had to deal with the results of my original choices. So please help me choose the right way— your way—the first time instead of taking the wrong path and getting caught up in sad consequences. I'm grateful I can ask for your help. I'm grateful you hear me. I'm grateful you love me. Wow, with those truths surrounding me, I realize I do have a bright future. Thank you.

Thoughts to Ponder

1. Have you ever had an attitude, or seen it in others, that said, "Thanks. I'll take it from here"? If so, what happened? If not, what has spared you, or others, from that experience?

2. Have you ever seen God's bright glory in the darkness of repeated problems? If so, what was the situation? If not, how would you like him to encourage you?
3. How do you handle occasions where you must be in the presence of those who make you uncomfortable? How would you like to act during those times? In what ways do you give yourself credit for your response?

Personal Ponderings

Sandra P. Aldrich is president and CEO of Bold Words, Inc. She is a well-known speaker and has appeared on such radio and TV programs as *Focus on the Family, The 700 Club, Prime Time America,* and many more. In addition to radio and TV appearances, she is a popular speaker throughout the United States and beyond. Her speaking venues cover a wide range from Women of Virtue conferences, women's and couple's retreats, college conferences, hospice seminars, and single parent events to business meetings and military bases. Always, she presents the serious issues of life with insight and humor. Sandra is the mother of two grown children and makes her home in Colorado.

Connect with

Sandra

and find additional resources at

sandraaldrich.com

Encouragement, Inspiration, and Wisdom from a Single Mom Who Has Been Where You Are

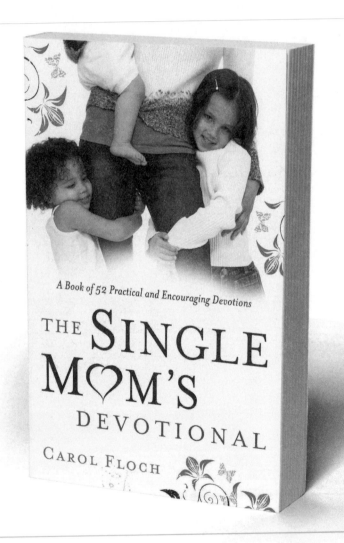

A Book of 52 Practical and Encouraging Devotions

THE SINGLE MOM'S DEVOTIONAL

CAROL FLOCH

Revell
a division of Baker Publishing Group
www.RevellBooks.com

Available Wherever Books and eBooks Are Sold

GOD IS ON YOUR SIDE
AND YOU'RE NOT ALONE

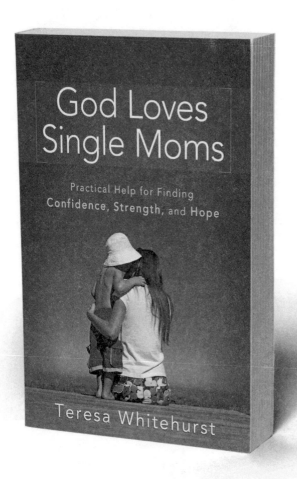

In *God Loves Single Moms*, Teresa offers you down-to-earth advice on navigating the world of single motherhood with confidence and hope for the future.

ℛ Revell
a division of Baker Publishing Group
www.RevellBooks.com

Available Wherever Books and eBooks Are Sold

Be the First to Hear about Other New Books from REVELL!

Sign up for announcements about new and upcoming titles at

RevellBooks.com/SignUp

Don't miss out on our great reads!

Revell

a division of Baker Publishing Group
www.RevellBooks.com